Contents

List of abbreviations   v

1 The Founding Fathers and civil rights   1

Introduction   1
Towards political equality   4
States' rights   6
The Civil War, 1861–65   9
Document case study   *11*

2 Reconstruction   14

Presidential Reconstruction   14
Congressional Reconstruction   17
Black Reconstruction   23
Document case study   *24*

3 Return of white supremacy   29

The Ku Klux Klan and other activists   29
Response of the African Americans   35
Document case study   *37*

4 Jim Crow   45

Decline in the rights of the African American   45
The 'Progressive' era   50
Document case study   *54*

5 Early black protest   58

Early black leaders   58
Organised black resistance   61
Document case study   *65*

6 Impact of war   70

The First World War   70
The inter-war period   75
The Second World War   76
Document case study   *77*

Contents

7 Civil rights in the Cold War   **82**

The motive for social reform   82
Truman and civil rights   82
Black initiatives   84
Legislation   88
Kennedy and civil rights   89
Johnson's 'Great Society'   94
Assassination of Martin Luther King Jr   98
Nixon and civil rights   99
Document case study   *100*

8 Other minority rights   **106**

Growth of the US nation   106
Immigration since 1945   111
Native Americans   114
Women's rights   116
The 'rights revolution'   119
Document case study   *120*

Conclusion   125
Select bibliography   127
Chronology   129
Index   134

Abbreviations

AFL-CIO	American Federation of Labor and Congress of Industrial Organizations
AIM	American Indian Movement
ASWPL	Association of Southern Women for the Prevention of Lynching
AWOC	Agricultural Workers Organizing Committee
BIA	Bureau of Indian Affairs
CBC	Congressional Black Caucus
CIC	Council for Interracial Co-operation
CILS	California Indian Legal Service
CORE	Congress of Racial Equality
EEOC	Equal Employment Opportunity Commission
ERA	Equal Rights Amendment
FEPC	Fair Employment Practice Commission
FOR	Fellowship of Reconciliation
MALDEF	Mexican American Legal Defense and Education Fund
NAACP	National Association for the Advancement of Colored People
NACW	National Association of Colored Women
NARF	Native American Rights Fund
NAWSA	National American Woman Suffrage Association
NFWA	National Farm Workers Association
NOW	National Organization for Women
OAAU	Organization of Afro-American Unity
ROAR	'Restore Our Alienated Rights'
SCLC	Southern Christian Leadership Conference
SNCC	Student Non-violent Co-ordinating Committee
UFWA	United Farm Workers of America
UFWOC	United Farm Workers Organizing Committee
UNIA	Universal Negro Improvement Association

The text in this book uses the term 'blacks' or 'African Americans' when referring to those of African descent. However, the sources provided sometimes contain different terms that were used at the time. Often these were used to offend or degrade people, but they are retained in these pages as they tell us something about the ideas and feelings of those who used them.

1   The Founding Fathers and civil rights

Introduction

The Declaration of Independence, signed by the original 13 United States of America on 4 July 1776, proclaimed: 'We hold these truths to be self-evident, that all men are created equal, that they are endowed by their Creator with certain unalienable rights, that among these are life, liberty, and the pursuit of happiness.' Yet as originally conceived by the Founding Fathers, who formed the wealthy minority of the new American republic, the 'unalienable rights' of the individual were enjoyed only by white, male, Protestant property holders. The rights of others – including Native Americans, American women of all ethnic backgrounds, members of non-Protestant religious denominations, and what became known in the twentieth century as minority ethnic groups – were not considered at that time.

As a result, the political philosophy within the original assertion of independence for Americans in 1776 was fraught with inconsistencies. These were to lead the new and vibrant young nation through over two hundred years of trial and tribulation in search for freedom and equality for all of its citizens. Along the way, the original inhabitants of the North American continent, the Native Americans, were to lose their hunting grounds and suffer the depredations of reservation life. African Americans fought and died for the independence of the new nation during the Revolutionary War and the war of 1812 – caused by naval interference with American shipping during the Royal Navy blockade of France – and then saw their own liberties gradually removed. A civil war was fought between 1861 and 1865; it resulted in 620,000 dead, but culminated in the 13th Amendment to the Constitution, which finally freed all slaves throughout the United States. A further hundred years would elapse during which African Americans suffered the terrible brutalities of the Ku Klux Klan, tolerated the indignation of the 'Jim Crow' laws, and finally gained full recognition as a result of the civil rights campaign of the 1960s.

The concept of civil rights

The concept of civil rights encompasses the belief that human beings have unalienable rights and liberties that cannot justly be violated by others or by the state. Linked to the history of democracy, the idea was first expressed by the philosophers of ancient Greece. Socrates (c.469–399 BC) chose to die rather than give up the right to speak his mind in the search for wisdom and truth. Prior to the rise of Christianity, the Stoic philosophers recognised and advocated the brotherhood of humanity and the natural equality of all human beings. The principles of personal liberty continued to be developed in the writings of the Roman statesman Marcus Tullius Cicero (106–43 BC) and the Greek essayist Plutarch (c.AD 46–120). Nevertheless, such ideas did not obtain a permanent place in the political structure of the Roman Empire and all but vanished during the Middle Ages.

Influenced by the revolutionary changes in thinking in the seventeenth century wrought by the Civil Wars, the Glorious Revolution, and William III's Declaration of Rights, British colonists carried the concepts of limited government and individual freedom to the New World. The events leading to the American and French revolutions of the eighteenth century inspired the work of the French philosophers Voltaire and Jean-Jacques Rousseau, and of the British reformer John Wilkes. Writings such as the *Declaration of Independence*, by Thomas Jefferson (1743–1826), and the *Declaration of the Rights of Man and of the Citizen*, composed principally by Abbé (later Count) Emmanuel Sieyès (1748–1836), formally laid the foundations for modern ideas of civil liberties.

The civil rights and liberties enjoyed by US citizens today are embodied in the Bill of Rights, which represents the first ten amendments to the US Constitution. Based on fear that a strong central government would lead to tyranny, this development was originally inspired by the actions of the Virginia and Massachusetts legislatures, both of which had incorporated a bill of rights into their original state constitutions in 1776 and 1780 respectively. These two states, with New York and Pennsylvania, refused to ratify the new Federal Constitution in 1787 unless it was amended to protect the individual with a similar bill of rights. In 1790 Congress submitted 12 amendments to the Constitution, 10 of which were adopted in 1791 as Articles I to X.

The 1st Amendment guaranteed freedom of speech, press, assembly, and religious exercise, as well as separation of church and state. The 2nd Amendment ensured that each state could form its own militia, while the 3rd Amendment regulated the manner in which soldiers could be billeted with civilians. The 4th Amendment protected the privacy and security of the home and personal effects, and prohibited unreasonable searches and seizures. The 5th to 8th Amendments guaranteed the right to trial by jury, the right to confront hostile witnesses and to have legal counsel, and the privilege of not testifying against oneself. The 5th Amendment also contained the all-important guarantee that no one shall be deprived of life, liberty, or property without due process of law. The 9th and 10th Amendments reserved to the people or to the states powers not allocated to the Federal government under the Constitution.

Slavery

But to the Americans who penned the Constitution in 1787, and the Bill of Rights in 1791, a stronger Federal government was the main objective. It was a means of overcoming the weaknesses inherent in the Articles of Confederation, drafted by

John Dickinson in 1776 and adopted in 1781, under which the 13 original states had been only loosely bound together in 'a Confederacy of States, each of which must have a separate government'.

The civil rights inherent within the Bill of Rights did not extend to everyone – particularly not to the 500,000 slaves resident in the United States by that time – hence the contradiction between document and deed. Thomas Jefferson, the main author of the declaration, referred to the slave trade as 'this infamous practice' in his instructions to the Virginia delegates in 1776, and even included a tirade against it in the first draft of the document. However, he permitted the offending clauses to be stricken out by the Continental Congress, the newly formed American system of government, commenting that it was done to please the Southern states of South Carolina and Georgia, 'who had never attempted to restrain the importation of slaves, and who, on the contrary, still wished to continue it'. Regarding the attitude of the Northern states, some of which had already abolished slavery, Jefferson remarked: 'Our Northern brethren, also, I believe, felt a little tender under these censures; for tho' their people have very few slaves themselves yet they have been pretty considerable carriers of them to others.'

Of slavery, George Washington, the first president of the United States, wrote: 'Among my first wishes is to see some plan adopted by which slavery in this country may be abolished.' The Virginia statesman Patrick Henry declared: 'I will not, I cannot justify it.' Benjamin Franklin became a leader of the Society for Promoting the Abolition of Slavery in Pennsylvania, and Alexander Hamilton, the first US secretary of the Treasury, helped to organise the New York Manumission Society, which raised funds to buy freedom for slaves.

Yet the men who met at Philadelphia to write a constitution for the new nation in 1787 came to build a stronger and more united country, not to solve the question of slavery. In order to retain the loyalty of slave holders and slave traders in the South and North, they promised to protect slave property in three separate sections of the Constitution. Firstly, they gave the small African slave trade 20 years in which to cease operations. After 1807 it would be illegal to import any further slaves into the country. The impact of this measure was minimal as the slave population within the United States had more than quadrupled by 1840. Secondly, via the passage of the Fugitive Slave Act of 1793 they provided that all runaway slaves be returned to their owners. Thirdly, because slave holders were to be taxed for their slaves, as property, they were permitted three votes for every five slaves they owned.

Despite having struck a bargain with those who traded in other human beings, the majority of delegates left the Constitutional Convention in 1787 convinced that slavery would eventually die out in America. This view was supported by the Northwest Ordinance, passed during the same year. Dealing with the settlement of territory beyond the 13 original states, this vital piece of legislature also prohibited slavery in what became Ohio, Indiana, Illinois, Michigan, and Wisconsin. Although the Federal government subsequently watered down this provision of the ordinance, insisting that it was merely a means of stopping the further importation of slaves, the five states did eventually abolish slavery. Encouraged by this, and by the fact that seven of the Northern states had already emancipated their slaves in one form or another, the 55 men who created the American Constitution felt sure that the compromises of 1787 were a temporary arrangement.

Entirely unforeseen was the invention of the cotton gin by Eli Whitney in 1793. A machine that solved the problem of separating the seeds from the fibres of upland or short-staple cotton, it made cotton-growing possible on almost any soil in regions with sufficient rainfall plus two hundred continuous frost-free days. Hence more slaves were needed on the new plantations that spread west into the fertile lands of Alabama, Mississippi, and eastern Texas. Instead of dying out by 1807, the slave trade had received fresh impetus. Ignoring the Constitution, merchants continued to import Africans and violated all legal efforts to halt the trade.

Towards political equality

Extension of white male suffrage

Throughout the first half of the nineteenth century, the acceleration of the economic development of the United States was accompanied by a growing demand among the white population for a more democratic society. By 1831 there were 24 states in the Union. Immigration was running at the rate of 60,000 a year, and the population had risen to 12 million. Throughout New England and Pennsylvania the textile and iron industries were beginning to provide employment for larger numbers of workers. Townships along the eastern seaboard steadily increased in size and in the range and scope of their economic activities. Transport and communications improved rapidly with the building of canals and railroads, while steamboats plied the Mississippi River and its tributaries.

Amidst this industrial revolution grew a desire for greater political equality. Property qualifications for voting in the older eastern states were gradually being replaced by the introduction of universal white manhood suffrage in the new western territories entering the Union after 1812. During this 'era of the common man', 28 per cent of the adult white, male electorate had gained the vote by 1828. By 1840, and following the period of 'Jacksonian Democracy' under President Andrew Jackson during the 1830s, this had risen to 70 per cent. In some Southern states the motive behind the extension of the vote was undoubtedly the desire to encourage support for slavery among the white population in the face of growing pressure from the abolitionists in the North.

Antebellum discrimination

Meanwhile, free blacks in both North and South had been guaranteed civil rights in return for service in the Continental Army raised to fight for American independence between 1775 and 1781. Instead, they saw these rights being eroded in the pre-Civil War, or antebellum, period during the first half of the nineteenth century. Most states disenfranchised blacks while extending the vote to whites. In 1802 Thomas Jefferson, by then the third president of the United States, signed a bill that excluded free blacks from the polls in the newly designated capital of Washington DC. Between 1790 and 1820 free blacks were also barred from jury service in every territory and in the District of Columbia. Blacks who had voted for years in Maryland, Tennessee, North Carolina, and Pennsylvania were barred from doing so in 1810, 1834, 1835, and 1838 respectively. Between 1819 and 1865, every new state granted suffrage to white males only. By 1840, 93 per cent of the small free black population of the United States had been disenfranchised.

During the same period, African Americans were excluded from the better-paid skilled trades. They were barred from the militia and, increasingly, from government service. They were also denied opportunities to expand westwards. To enter the territory of Iowa in 1839 blacks had to present a $500 bond and proof that they were free. Few had such proof and even fewer had $500. By 1844 Iowans announced that they would 'never consent to open the doors of our beautiful state' to people of colour, for equality would lead to 'discord and violence'. Two years later Iowa entered the Union as a free state, but prejudices remained.

On the political scene, support for civil rights began to fail as the two-party system disintegrated. Until the 1840s the Democratic and Whig parties had each drawn support from North and South. But as Southern commitment to the 'peculiar institution' of slavery grew, and opposition to it developed elsewhere, the parties inevitably began to reform along sectional, or North–South, lines. Most significantly, the Democrats had by 1844 omitted the Declaration of Independence from their party political platform, and consequently began to win back the wealthy cotton planters who had been part of the Whig coalition. The civil rights of US citizens were sacrificed for the sake of party unity.

Missouri Compromise of 1820

The first large-scale intrusion of the slavery issue into American politics occurred in 1817, by which time there were 22 states in the Union, of which half were free and half were slave. In that year the territorial legislature of Missouri, a section of the Louisiana Purchase which was part of 828,000 square miles of territory in the mid west purchased from France in 1803, applied to Congress for admission to the Union. Settled mainly by Southerners by 1817, Missouri had 66,000 inhabitants, 6,000 of them slaves. Its application to Congress threatened to upset the balance of free and slave states in the Union. Supporters of the constitution proposed for the state were happy therefore to recognise and protect slavery.

Northern opposition to this development crystallised on 13 February 1819, when Representative James Tallmadge, of New York, introduced an amendment to the Missouri constitution that would prohibit the further introduction of slaves into the state, and provide for the gradual emancipation of slaves already there. Northerners like Tallmadge wished to bar slavery from the entire mid west because emigrants from free states were unwilling to settle in slave areas.

The debate that followed spanned two sessions of Congress and came, the ageing Thomas Jefferson wrote, 'like a fireball in the night', which 'awakened me and filled me with terror. I considered it at once the knell of the union.' To another former US president, John Quincy Adams, it seemed to be 'a title page to a great tragic volume'. The main question of the debate was whether Congress had the right to regulate slavery in territories applying for admission as states.

The nation was eventually calmed in 1820 by the moderation of Whig senator Henry Clay, of Kentucky. Clay offered a compromise which permitted Missouri to be admitted to the Union as a slave state on 10 August 1821, whilst Maine – hitherto part of Massachusetts – would come into the Union as a free state on 15 May 1820. Furthermore, a demarcation line would be drawn from east to west at latitude 36 degrees 30 minutes north of the equator. The eastern end of this invisible line ran along the Mason-Dixon line established by Charles Mason and Jeremiah Dixon, who had surveyed and mapped it in the 1760s to settle a border dispute between the colonies of Pennsylvania and Maryland. Henceforth, all new states created from Louisiana Purchase territory north of that line would be free, while those below it would be permitted to hold slaves.

The Missouri Compromise glossed over the problem of the extension of slavery, and was satisfactory to no one. This was the first time in American history that an action by Congress had aligned the states against each other on a sectional basis. It led to increased suspicion on both sides, and foretold what lay ahead. At very best, the Missouri Compromise gave the United States about 25 years of reasonably peaceful internal growth, but the ultimate price for this was paid during the Civil War from 1861 to 1865.

States' rights

Historians have argued at length about whether the states have the constitutional right to secede, or break away, from the Union. According to one interpretation, the Constitution was a compact between sovereign states that retained all the powers not specifically surrendered to the Federal government. This was implied in the 10th Amendment. Furthermore, as nothing was mentioned about secession in the Constitution, it might be regarded by Southerners as one of the reserved powers. On the other hand, the Constitution had been framed by the people of the United States to form 'a more perfect Union' and hence was a binding contract that could not be broken.

The first real test regarding the rights of the various states to secede from the Union came in 1832 during the 'nullification crisis', which was caused by a series of acts imposing duties on American imports. The Tariff of 1816 introduced the principle of protection in order to safeguard the infant industries of the United States from British competition, and had received general approval because the South as well as the North expected to develop industry. This expectation was not fully realised. While the North built up new industries at a phenomenal rate, the South remained mainly agricultural. It exported large quantities of cotton to

England and imported necessary manufactured goods. On 19 May 1828 'an act in alteration of the several acts imposing duties on imports', which the South called the 'Tariff of Abominations', was passed by the government of Andrew Jackson. It increased duties on goods coming into the United States.

The nullification crisis finally came to a head after the passage on 14 July 1832 of yet another Tariff Act, which was designed to decrease pressure on the South by reducing existing rates slightly. But South Carolina was by this time in no mood to be appeased. Led by John C. Calhoun, who resigned as vice-president in order to fight for Southern rights on the floor of the Senate, the state responded by declaring the Tariffs of 1828 and 1832 'null and void' via an ordinance passed on 29 November 1832. The state also threatened to secede from the Union if the Federal government attempted to collect customs duties within its borders.

There followed a period of posturing and military preparation on the part of both the government in Washington DC and the state of South Carolina, during which Jackson threatened to enact a 'force bill' empowering him to use the armed forces to collect customs duties in South Carolina. A compromise was reached when Henry Clay ('the great pacificator'), in liaison with Calhoun, suggested a measure providing for the gradual reduction of all tariffs over a nine-year period to a uniform level of 20 per cent, which by 1842 would bring rates down to 1816 levels. The Force Bill and the Compromise Tariff were simultaneously passed by Congress and approved by Jackson on 1 March 1833. This compromise was accepted by the South Carolina Convention on 15 March 1833, after which the state withdrew its nullification ordinance but defiantly nullified the Force Act – a face-saving gesture that Jackson chose to ignore.

Thus both sides claimed victory, with Jackson declaring that no state could defy Federal authority with impunity, whilst South Carolina had been able to change Federal policy. Civil war had been averted, but the fundamental issues of states' rights, nullification, and secession remained unsolved.

Compromise of 1850

The issue of states' rights, slavery, and secession came to a head again in 1849. As a result of the American defeat of Mexico between 1846 and 1848, and territory subsequently being ceded to the United States, California and New Mexico were admitted to the Union as free states. This development angered the South as the admission of both territories as free states would upset the sectional balance in the Senate, the number of free and slave states still being equal up to that time – 15 of each. With a lack of control in the House of Representatives, and little prospect of any of the remaining territories being admitted to the Union as slave states, the South reacted by threatening to leave the Union. South Carolina and Mississippi, the two states with the largest slave populations, led the movement. A Southern rights convention met at Nashville, Tennessee, in June 1850 to consider the possibility of secession. After a seven-month debate in Congress, Henry Clay once again suggested a compromise. It included an improved fugitive slave law. This resulted in the Compromise of 1850, and once more the break-up of the Union was averted.

Kansas–Nebraska crisis

The uneasy truce established between North and South in 1850 was brought to an end in January 1854 by a measure introduced to Congress by Stephen A. Douglas, a Democratic senator from Illinois. In his capacity as chairman of the Senate Committee on Territories, Douglas organised a bill to provide civil government to a huge area of territory in the Nebraska country, an area of the Great Plains lying west of Iowa and Missouri which stretched north to the Canadian border and west to the Rocky Mountains. An amendment to the bill subsequently divided this area into two separate territories called Kansas and Nebraska. As both of these territories lay north of the 36 degrees 30 minutes line of latitude, it was assumed by many that they would be free of slavery, as stipulated by the Missouri Compromise of 1820. But the Douglas Bill, reported from the Senate Committee on Territories on 4 January 1854, provided that the question of slavery in these territories would be settled by 'popular sovereignty', that is by the people of Kansas and Nebraska. A further amendment to the bill, introduced by Senator Dixon of Kentucky, recommended the repeal of the Missouri Compromise. Hoping for Southern support in his attempt to run for president, Douglas accepted Dixon's measure.

After a five-month debate, the Kansas–Nebraska Act finally became law in May 1854 by a narrow margin of 113 to 100. In the North the repeal of the Missouri Compromise caused a storm of popular anger, and Douglas was condemned as a traitor. The division caused by the passage of this Act shattered political party lines. Every Northern Whig had opposed the bill, while nearly every Southern Whig supported it. All the Southern Democrats voted for it, whilst the Northern Democrats were split, with 44 in favour and 43 against it. Thus sectionalism had virtually destroyed the Whig Party, and was beginning to undermine the Democrats. The Kansas–Missouri Border War that erupted in 1856 between free-soil and pro-slavery elements who flooded westwards was further proof that the American nation was on a collision course.

Formation of the anti-slavery Republican Party

The years 1854–56 witnessed a period of flux and change on the American political landscape as new parties rose in response to the times. Opposition to the passage of the Kansas–Nebraska Act resulted in the organisation of a new political party pledged to oppose the further extension of slavery in the territories. The new Republican Party was organised by the merger of the remnants of the Liberty Party, formed in 1840 to secure the abolition of slavery; the Free Soil Party, launched in 1848 to oppose the extension of slavery; the Northern Whigs, who were discouraged by their party's indecision on the slavery issue; and anti-slavery Democrats, called 'Barnburners', who were angered by the Kansas–Nebraska Act.

At Ripon, Wisconsin, on 28 February 1854, a small group of people representing these various factions met to express their outrage over the Kansas–Nebraska Bill, and adopted a motion to call themselves Republicans. The Republicans soon began to draw support from the North and the west – which together possessed most of the nation's population; much of its food supply; and the bulk of its industry, commerce, and railroads. During the presidential election of 1856, which saw the election of Democrat James Buchanan, the Republicans nominated as their candidate the explorer John C. Frémont, whose surname lent itself to the popular slogan 'Free soil, Free speech, Free men and Frémont'. Carrying only 11 out of 16 free-soil states, their platform predictably denounced the Kansas–Nebraska Act and demanded that Congress prohibit slavery in that territory.

The 'John Brown' rebellion

In 1859 a fanatical white abolitionist called John Brown, who had already made his mark by murdering several pro-slavery settlers during the Kansas–Missouri Border War in 1856, attempted to start a slave rebellion by seizing the government armoury at Harper's Ferry, Virginia. The slaves did not rise, but angry townsfolk did – surrounding Brown's small 'freedom army', which sought refuge in the town fire-engine house. This building was eventually stormed by 90 US Marines led by Robert E. Lee, who later commanded the Confederate Army during the Civil War. Brown was wounded and captured, and nine of his followers were killed – including two of his sons and two blacks. John Brown and his accomplices were publicly hanged at Charles Town, Virginia, during November that year. Although many Northerners disapproved of Brown's methods, his attempted rebellion at Harper's Ferry persuaded many people that slavery in the US had to be abolished, and convinced many Southerners that slavery had to be defended.

The Civil War, 1861–65

The final straw for the South came in 1860, when Abraham Lincoln was elected the first Republican president on a platform of hostility to the expansion of slavery. The reaction in South Carolina was swift. On 20 December a special state convention unanimously passed an ordinance of secession that dissolved 'the Union now subsisting between South Carolina and other States'. The ordinance passed by South Carolina was concerned wholly with ways in which the North had violated the constitutional rights of slave holders. During January and February 1861 six other cotton states – Mississippi, Florida, Alabama, Georgia, Louisiana, and Texas – followed suit and seceded from the Union, forming themselves into short-lived republics. Finally, on 4 February, the seven seceded states met at Montgomery, Alabama, in order to draw up a constitution and choose a president for the Confederate States of America. They were joined by Virginia, Arkansas, Tennessee, and North Carolina, four slave states in the Upper South. The break-up of the Union was complete, and the possibility of achieving freedom and civil rights for all in America seemed more remote than ever.

The abolition of slavery was not the sole cause of the Civil War that began with the bombardment of Fort Sumter, in Charleston Harbor, during April 1861. In fact, most Northerners were not abolitionists and discriminated against blacks as readily as many in the South. Furthermore, factory and mill owners in the North feared a rise in the cost of Southern goods if the plantation owners were forced to pay wages to freed African Americans, while Northern factory workers were afraid that freed slaves would deprive them of jobs by toiling for lower wages. However, the struggle to free the slaves had superseded these political and economic considerations by 1863 to become the major reason why fellow Americans were at war.

At the beginning of the conflict, African Americans who escaped across the battle lines, or were liberated by invading Union armies, were treated with contempt and treated as 'contraband of war' – that is as captured enemy property. Throughout 1861–62 blacks were used by both sides merely as a labour force to build fortifications and to man-handle the munitions of war. But towards the end of 1862 there was a growing awareness that a Union army with African-American soldiers in its ranks might have a greater motivation to win the Civil War. The large-scale recruitment of black troops was mainly the work of ex-slave Frederick Douglass, self-educated lawyer John M. Langston, and Martin Delany, a doctor who later became an officer in the Union Army. During the last three years of the conflict, black Northern regiments took part in more than 30 major battles. Of the 178,892 African Americans who fought for the Union, 32,369 – more than a sixth of their number – died in uniform.

At the same time, President Lincoln faced increasing pressure from the abolitionists to emancipate the slaves, at least in the Confederate states. On 17 September 1862 the Union Army at last achieved a partial victory, when it stopped General Robert E. Lee's army at Antietam in Maryland. Lincoln then felt strong enough to issue the Emancipation Proclamation, which proclaimed that if any state (or part of a state) was still in rebellion by New Year's Day 1863, the slaves there would be 'forever free'. With the arrival of the deadline not a single Southern state had re-entered the Union. Meanwhile, the slaves in the border states of Maryland, Kentucky, and Missouri were unaffected by the proclamation. As a result, Lincoln's edict had failed to free a single slave. None the less, the Emancipation Proclamation extended the nation's commitment to freedom and set in motion the events that finally brought about the legal abolition of slavery via the 13th Amendment to the Constitution in 1865. But little did the four million black Americans whose lives were transformed by the passage of this measure realise that it would take over a hundred years of struggle to secure fully their civil rights as American citizens. The following chapters examine this struggle, along with that of the other minority groups in the United States.

The Founding Fathers and civil rights

1.1 Congressman William Eustis describes the role of African Americans in the Revolutionary War

At the commencement of the Revolutionary War, there were found in the Middle and Northern States, many blacks, and other people of color, capable of bearing arms; a part of them free, the greater part slaves. The freemen entered our ranks with the whites. The time of those who were slaves was purchased by the states; and they were induced to enter the service in consequence of a law, by which, on condition of their serving in the ranks during the war, they were made freemen. In Rhode Island, where their numbers were more considerable, they were formed, under the same considerations, into a regiment commanded by white officers; and it is required, in justice to them, to add, that they discharged their duty with zeal and fidelity . . .

The war over, and peace restored, these men returned to their respective states; and who could have said to them, on their return to civil life, after having shed their blood in common with the whites in the defense of the liberties of the country: 'You are not to participate in the rights secured by the struggle, or in the liberty for which you have been fighting'? Certainly no white man in Massachusetts.

Source: George Livermore, *An historical research respecting the opinions of the founders of the republic on negroes as slaves, as citizens and as soldiers*, Annals of Congress, 16th Congress, 2nd Session, Boston, 1862, p. 154

1.2 Students at Lane Seminary, near Cincinnati, Ohio, report on the conditions under which free blacks lived in that city in 1834

A respectable master mechanic stated to us . . . that in 1830 the President of the Mechanical Association was publicly tried by the Society for the crime of assisting a colored young man to learn a trade. Such was the feeling among the mechanics that no colored boy could learn a trade, or colored journeyman find employment. A young man of exceptional character and an excellent workman purchased his freedom and learned the cabinet making business in Kentucky. On coming to this city, he was refused work by every man to whom he applied. At last he found a shop carried on by an Englishman, who agreed to employ him—but on entering the shop, the workmen threw down their tools and declared that he should leave or they would . . . The unfortunate youth was accordingly dismissed.

In this extremity, having spent his last cent, he found a slave-holder who gave him employment in an iron store as a common laborer. Here he remained two years, when the gentleman finding he was a mechanic, exerted his influence and procured work for him as a rough carpenter. This man, by dint of perseverance and industry, has now become a master workman, employing at times six or eight journeymen. But, he tells us, he has not yet received a single job of work from a native born citizen of a free state.

Source: *Proceedings of Ohio Anti-slavery Convention*, Cincinnati, 1835, p. 19

1.3 Ex-slave Dr James W. C. Pennington protests against segregation on a horse-drawn streetcar in New York in 1856

. . . as the doctor took his seat on the right side of the car, the [white] passengers near him rose up and left a vacant space on both sides of him for three or four seats. A number of the passengers went to the conductor and requested him to turn Dr. P. out. [Pennington denied this.] He was approached and asked civilly to take a seat on the front platform, as that was the regulation on the road. He declined, but the conductor insisted on his leaving his seat to which he replied that he would maintain his rights . . .

The conductor then asked the driver to stop the car, and remove the doctor. He stopped, took Dr. P. in his arms, embraced him, and carried him backward through the car, the doctor apparently making all the resistance in his power. He was, however, forced through the car, over the platform and into the street, near the sidewalk.

Source: *New York Daily Tribune*, 19 December 1856

1.4 Letter published in South Carolina in 1832, entitled 'Now's the time & now the hour to strike for liberty'

. . . Less than 50 years have passed away, and the sovereign *rights* which our fathers achieved for Carolina, by their blood, are *called into question*. We must maintain those rights THIS DAY, or we are lost forever. We shall be brought back to a state of 'colonial vassalage,' certainly not less acceptable from the reflection that we will have 'forged the chains' ourselves, with which our liberties will be manacled.—What, my countrymen, is THE QUESTION now to be decided? Is it not whether South Carolina shall give up the glorious contest for our rights, in which we have been engaged for eight years past, and be reduced to 'unconditional submission?' or maintain that contest with all her heart, and mind, and soul? . . . Are we not struggling to maintain the CONSTITUTION, which has been perverted by Congress to the unholy purpose of levying contributions upon the South, that the North and West may 'divide the spoils?'

Source: *Charleston Mercury* (South Carolina), 3 September 1832

1.5 President Abraham Lincoln's letter of 26 August 1863 in response to a Union Army officer opposed to freeing the slaves and using them as soldiers

I know, as fully as one can know the opinions of others, that some of the commanders of our armies in the field, who have given us our most important success, believe the emancipation policy and the use of the colored troops constitute the heaviest blow yet dealt to the rebellion, and that at least one of these important successes could not have been achieved when it was but for the aid of black soldiers . . . You say you will not fight to free Negroes. Some of them seem willing to fight for you—but no matter. Fight you, then, exclusively to save the Union. Whenever you shall have conquered all resistance to the Union, if I shall urge you to continue fighting, it will be an apt time then for you to declare you will not fight to free Negroes . . . I thought that whatever Negroes can be got to do as soldiers leaves just so much less for white soldiers to do in saving the Union. Does it appear otherwise to you? But Negroes, like other people, act upon motives. Why should they do anything for us, if we will do nothing for them? If they stake their lives for us, they must be prompted by the strongest motives, even the promise of freedom. And the promise, being made, must be kept . . .

Source: John G. Nicolay and John Hay, *Abraham Lincoln, A history*, vol. 7, New York, 1904, pp. 382–84

Document case-study questions

1 To what extent do you think the view expressed by Congressman William Eustis in Document 1.1 regarding civil rights might be representative of all African Americans by 1850?

2 What does Document 1.2 tell you about the attitude towards skilled free blacks in the antebellum United States?

3 Explain how the conductor and driver in Document 1.3 might have justified their actions in a free state in the 1850s.

4 In what ways does Document 1.4 explain the position the state of South Carolina adopted regarding states' rights in 1832?

5 What reasons does President Abraham Lincoln give in Document 1.5 for recruiting African Americans into the Union Army?

2 Reconstruction

Presidential Reconstruction

On 15 April 1865 Vice-President Andrew Johnson was unexpectedly sworn in as president of the United States of America amidst the tears and confusion of a nation. During the days of mourning that followed the assassination of Abraham Lincoln, many within the Republican Party expected Johnson to impose a harsh reconstruction programme on the defeated South. Although a Southerner, he had remained loyal to the Union during the Civil War, and was appointed military governor of Tennessee from 1862 to 1864. During this time, he worked amicably with the Radical Republicans, who criticised Lincoln for failing to make the emancipation of the slaves a war goal and later for being too eager to readmit the conquered Southern states into the Union. Indeed, Johnson had taken a strong anti-Confederate stance, declaring: 'Treason must be made odious, and traitors must be punished and impoverished.'

Hence, many Republicans were shocked when Johnson announced his 'Presidential Reconstruction' plan in May 1865, with Congress out of session and not due to reconvene until December of that year. Presented as a continuation of Lincoln's moderate wartime reconstruction policy, Johnson's plan was, in fact, very much his own. A self-educated man of humble North Carolina origins, he neither adopted abolitionist ideals nor challenged racist sentiment. Instead, he held a life-long hatred of the planter aristocracy, and hoped that an end to slavery would hasten the demise of those Southern aristocrats.

Meanwhile, Democratic opposition within Congress to the abolition of slavery was overcome on 31 January 1865, and the 13th Amendment to the US Constitution was finally ratified on 6 December of that year. Section One of this amendment stated: 'Neither slavery nor involuntary servitude, except as a punishment for crime whereof the party shall have been duly convicted, shall exist within the United States, or any place subject to their jurisdiction.' Although this measure did not cure the ills of racism and discrimination, it did for the first time make slavery illegal throughout the whole of the United States.

Concern for the well-being of blacks was not the only consideration of the Presidential Reconstruction programme. In a letter to Congress written two days before ratification of the 13th Amendment, Johnson remarked that he felt slavery impeded interstate commerce by creating different labour markets in slave and non-slave states. 'Slavery,' he stated, 'was essentially a monopoly of labour, and as such locked the states where it prevailed against the incoming of free industry.'

Presidential Reconstruction took effect during the summer of 1865. One of Johnson's first acts in office was to permit whites to reclaim all land given to blacks during the Civil War. On 29 May 1865 he extended a general pardon to former Confederates (known to their critics as 'White-washed Rebels') who were willing to take the oath of allegiance. Those who had held high office in the Confederacy, or whose taxable property exceeded $20,000 in value, were excluded but could obtain a special pardon via individual petition to the president. The four former Confederate states of Virginia, Louisiana, Arkansas, and Tennessee – which had already accepted Lincoln's plan permitting admission back into the Union after only 10 per cent of the male voting population had taken the oath of allegiance – were quickly recognised by Johnson. He appointed provisional governments for the remaining seven states, which were instructed to call constitutional conventions to be elected by those qualified to vote, that is those who had taken the oath. Preliminary to readmittance to the Union, these conventions were to withdraw their state's ordinance of secession of 1860–61, repudiate the Confederate and state war debts, and ratify the pending 13th Amendment. Following these measures, the Southern states might elect governments and representatives to the US Congress. Johnson left suffrage qualifications to individual states, though he did invite them to give the vote to a few qualified African Americans.

White Southerners responded only grudgingly to Johnson's Reconstruction plan. Some states merely repealed the ordinance of secession without rejecting it. Nearly all objected to the ratification of the 13th Amendment, while none took up Johnson's recommendation that there should be limited black suffrage. In both state and Federal elections, they defiantly chose prominent ex-Confederates. The first Southern representatives elected after the Civil War included 58 ex-Confederate congressmen, 6 ex-Confederate cabinet members, 9 ex-Confederate Army officers, and Alexander H. Stephens, ex-vice-president of the Confederacy.

Black Codes

Most significantly, Southern legislatures passed a series of laws in 1865 and 1866 called the Black Codes. Intended to replace the 'Slave Codes' which once regulated slavery, these laws originated partially in the antebellum legislature concerning free blacks, and in the freedmen's codes of the British West Indies. Designed to keep the freed black person in a subordinate position, they bestowed certain rights upon the African American; for instance he could make contracts, own property, sue in court, go to school, and enter into legal marriage. However, blacks were generally prohibited from voting or serving on juries. They could not own or carry guns, or testify against white people in court. They were made liable to heavier penalties for law breaking than were whites. They were forbidden to marry white people, and were excluded from occupations where they might be in competition with whites.

These restrictions were supplemented by other legislation. A black person in South Carolina needed a licence for any job other than farmer or servant, and the licence cost $100. Hence, most blacks were restricted to agriculture and domestic work. Mississippi had the most unrelenting code in the South. Blacks could not rent land in rural areas, which guaranteed a cheap labour force for white planters. To avoid punishment, black labourers had to be in possession of a worker's contract, thereby proving employment, by January for the following planting season. If a labourer left a job before his contract ended, all wages earned up to that point were forfeited. The Southern states required railroads to provide separate accommodation for blacks, thus establishing the precedent for segregation in public facilities. An education law specifically excluded them from sharing in the public school fund.

Finally, blacks were subject to vagrancy laws. An unemployed black apprehended and convicted, and unable to pay the fine, could be hired out to a planter or other employer. Indeed, members of the 74th United States Colored Infantry were arrested by the local Southern authorities the day after their discharge from the Federal Army because they did not have employment certificates.

A new form of slavery had replaced the old. Before the passage of the 13th Amendment, slaves had been the property of individual owners. As one Southerner noted towards the end of 1865, now 'the community as a whole controls the blacks as a group'.

Race riots

The introduction of Presidential Reconstruction was followed by the eruption of race riots in Memphis, Tennessee, and New Orleans, Louisiana. During the Civil War, the black population in Memphis had quadrupled and racial tensions were high. The riot there was sparked off on 1 May 1866 when the carriages of a black man and a white man collided. As a group of veterans of the 3rd US Colored Infantry tried to intervene to stop the arrest of the black man, a crowd of whites gathered at the scene. Fighting broke out, then escalated into three days of racially motivated violence, primarily pitting the police – who were mainly Irish Americans – against black residents. A total of 46 blacks died, and 85 were wounded. Five black women were raped, and hundreds of black homes, schools, and churches were broken into or destroyed by fire. Lucy Tibbs, the pregnant wife of a black riverboat man, was one of the victims. Testifying before the Joint Committee of Fifteen on Reconstruction, she stated: 'Just where I live, when the greatest fight was going on . . . there were, I should think, four hundred persons in the crowd. They were just firing at every colored man and boy they could see.'[1] The Joint Committee of Fifteen described the affair as 'an organized and bloody massacre of the colored people of Memphis, regardless of age, sex, or condition, inspired by the teachings of the press, and led on by sworn officers of the law composing the city government, and others'.[2]

Further racially motivated violence occurred when a Republican organisation called the Convention of 1864 – composed mainly of blacks, plus some white

Republicans – held a gathering in New Orleans on 30 July 1866. The white city authorities were opposed to the meeting, and planned to break it up. In order to provoke trouble, Mayor John T. Monroe withdrew his policemen from the streets, supplied them with revolvers, and kept them waiting at their station-houses for the signal to attack. He also misled the local military commander, Major General A. Blair, as to the hour of the meeting, so that he could not call out his troops in time to repress the trouble. Fighting broke out as a procession of about 140 blacks belonging to the Convention of 1864 marched towards the Mechanic's Institute; the police, followed by firemen and ex-Confederate soldiers, charged into the fray. There were 34 blacks killed, and 119 wounded. Major General Philip H. Sheridan, who commanded the Department of the Gulf, reported that the New Orleans riot was 'an absolute massacre by the police . . . a murder which the Mayor and Police of the city perpetrated without the shadow of a necessity'.[3]

Both of these riots helped undermine the viability of and support for President Johnson's lenient Reconstruction programme, which encouraged ex-Confederates back into power and ignored numerous racist outrages committed throughout the South.

Congressional Reconstruction

A struggle between Andrew Johnson and Congress began when the latter reassembled in December 1865 and refused to seat the representatives of the reorganised Southern states. The main opposition to Johnson came from the Radical Republicans. Forming the Joint Committee of Fifteen, they were determined to punish the Southern states and support the newly freed black people. Although chaired by William Pitt Fessenden, a mild-mannered statesman from Maine, the committee's dominant figure was the Pennsylvanian Thaddeus Stevens, while others included Senator Charles Sumner of Massachusetts and Secretary of the Treasury Salmon P. Chase. The leader of the Republicans in the House of Representatives, Thaddeus Stevens believed that the former Confederate states should be treated as a conquered nation and forced to pay the cost of the Civil War. The Joint Committee of Fifteen was strongly opposed to President Johnson's lenient Reconstruction policies towards the South. Despite Johnson's attempts at veto, they managed to pass a series of radical Acts through Congress between 1866 and 1870.

The Civil Rights Act of 9 April 1866 declared blacks citizens of the United States and guaranteed them the same protection of the law as white people. This Act was consolidated by the 14th Amendment to the US Constitution. Passed through Congress during June 1866, and finally ratified in 1868, the 14th Amendment declared in its first clause that all persons born or naturalised in the United States were citizens of the nation and citizens of their states. Furthermore, no state could abridge these rights without due process of law, or deny equal protection of the law.

Secondly, the 14th Amendment guaranteed that if a state denied suffrage to any of its male citizens its representation in Congress would be proportionally reduced. Although this clause could not guarantee black suffrage, it did threaten to deprive Southern states of some legislators if black men were denied the vote.

Thirdly, this amendment disqualified from state and national office all pre-war office holders who had supported the Confederacy, unless Congress removed their disqualification by a two-thirds majority vote. By this means, the Radical Republicans intended to counteract Johnson's wholesale distribution of pardons and amnesties. Finally, the amendment maintained the validity of the Federal war debt, but repudiated the Confederate war debt and, significantly, made ratification of the 14th Amendment a prerequisite for the admission of ex-Confederate states to the Union.

Military Reconstruction Act, 1867

With the exception of Tennessee, all the former Confederate states rejected the 14th Amendment. Therefore, Congress suspended the Southern governments recognised by President Lincoln and President Johnson, and passed the Military Reconstruction Act on 2 March 1867. Designed to replace Presidential Reconstruction with a far more stringent plan, this Act temporarily divided the former Confederacy, except Tennessee, into five military districts to be governed by generals of the US Army. These officers had the option to send offenders to local civil tribunals, or to organise military committees or tribunals for that purpose. For example, in one case tried via martial law in the Second Military District, the captain of the steamer *Pilot Boy* was found guilty and fined $250 for refusing to allow blacks to travel in his boat. In the same district, a black girl who defended herself when attacked by a white girl was taken from her school house by five white men and given 146 lashes. All five men were convicted and given jail sentences.

The 1867 Reconstruction Act also called for the election of constitutional conventions with blacks as well as whites being eligible to vote for delegates, but with ex-Confederate leaders barred. Furthermore, the Southern states were to ratify the 14th Amendment. They were also required to frame new constitutions extending suffrage to blacks, which were to be submitted to Congress for approval. By June 1868 seven of the ex-Confederate states had ratified the 14th Amendment and were duly readmitted to the Union via the Omnibus Act, although Georgia was promptly returned to military rule for refusing to comply.

The military occupation of the South caused bitter resentment among white Democrats. White Republicans who co-operated with the Federal troops became known as 'Scalawags', while those Northerners who came south, either as businessmen for personal gain or to improve living conditions and to educate the newly liberated blacks, were called 'Carpetbaggers'.

The 15th Amendment, 1869

The 15th Amendment to the Constitution, which was passed through Congress in February 1869, prohibited the denial of suffrage to all adult males because of 'race, color, or previous condition of servitude'. Although it was ratified by the remaining four ex-Confederate states, many Southern Democrats criticised this amendment for being designed to secure black votes for the Republican Party. Other Southerners contended that its omissions made it acceptable. As one Richmond newspaper commented, it had 'loopholes through which a coach and four horses can be driven'.[4] These loopholes included the lack of guarantee that blacks could be office holders, and no control over the introduction of voting restrictions such as property requirements and literacy tests. Ultimately, such restrictions were used to disastrous effect, denying blacks their right to vote.

Second Civil Rights Act, 1875

A further attempt to prevent segregation in public places was also thwarted. A second Civil Rights Act was introduced by Charles Sumner and Benjamin Butler in 1870, but this did not become law until 1 March 1875. The most sweeping piece of civil rights legislation before 1964, this promised that all persons – regardless of race, colour, or previous condition of servitude – were entitled to full and equal accommodation in 'inns, public conveyances on land or water, theatres, and other places of public amusement'. In 1883 the Supreme Court declared this Act to be unconstitutional and asserted that Congress did not have the power to regulate the conduct and transactions of individuals. On 31 May 1870 and 28 February 1871 respectively, Enforcement Acts were passed in order to provide for the protection of black voters and Federal supervision of Southern elections. A third Enforcement Act, passed in April 1871, also known as the Ku-Klux Act, dealt with a far more ominous threat to black civil rights (see Chapter 3).

Freedmen's Bureau

The Bureau of Refugees, Freedmen and Abandoned Lands, part of the War Department, was first established by Act of Congress on 3 March 1865. More commonly known as the Freedmen's Bureau, it was initially created for a period of one year after the close of the Civil War. Despite President Johnson's attempts at veto, a supplementary Act passed in July 1866 gave the Freedmen's Bureau a final form by extending its existence to at least 1870.

General Oliver O. Howard was placed in charge of the bureau's activities, and hundreds of army officers were assigned to departments throughout the South. Supported by civilian agents, they were charged in particular with the responsibility of aiding freed blacks to adjust to their new circumstances. For example, Captain Thomas W. Conway was appointed superintendent of freedmen, Department of the Gulf, on 19 April 1865, initially taking charge of the freedmen around Mobile, Alabama. The same army orders which appointed Conway announced: 'All persons formerly held as slaves will be treated in every respect as entitled to the rights of Freedmen, and such as desire their services will be required to pay for them.'[5]

The work of the bureau involved the development of educational and medical facilities, the administration of justice in law-suits involving freed people, and the provision of relief for both races. From 1865 to 1870 the bureau established

This engraving by A. R. Waud, published in *Harper's Weekly* on 25 July 1868, symbolised the work of the Freedmen's Bureau. A bureau official stands between ex-Confederate soldiers and freedmen in an attempt to prevent bloodshed.

approximately 4,500 schools and hired 9,500 teachers. Freed people of all ages flocked into the classroom. According to black spokesman Booker T. Washington, 'It was a whole race trying to go to school.' Bureau official John W. Alvord described the following scene in a North Carolina school in 1866: 'A child six years old, her mother, grandmother and great-grandmother, the latter over 75 years of age . . . commenced their alphabet together and each one can read the Bible fluently.'[6]

Some of the greatest educational successes of the Freedmen's Bureau were achieved in New Orleans. In January 1871, after two years of legal battles following the adoption of the 1868 Louisiana constitution, which called for integrated schools, black children entered 21 desegregated institutions, about one-third of the city's public schools. At the height of integration, between five hundred and a thousand blacks and several thousand whites attended mixed schools. Of the three public high schools, two were desegregated. Historian Louis R. Harlan has written that this experiment with integrated schools, which ended abruptly in 1877, was an experience shared by no other Southern community until after 1954, and by few Northern communities at the time.

Regarding health care, the bureau created over a hundred hospitals providing medical aid for half a million patients, and distributed over 20 million items of food to the destitute. The labour system of the South also had to be completely restructured after the Civil War. Many former slave owners attempted to trick former slaves into entering contracts on the same terms as under the slavery system. The Freedmen's Bureau acted on behalf of blacks to negotiate fair contracts for labour and property.

As regards the administration of justice, the civil courts in most Southern states refused to receive the testimony of blacks. The bureau attempted to overcome this by establishing provost courts for freedmen which were operated by the US Army. Empowered with the 'exclusive jurisdiction in all cases involving the rights of person or property of colored persons', these courts were almost immediately made powerless via a Supreme Court ruling which decreed that a military tribunal had no jurisdiction where a civil court was functioning in times of peace (see Chapter 4).[7]

During the Civil War, Union General William T. Sherman had permitted liberated blacks to be settled on abandoned plantations on the Sea Islands off South Carolina and Georgia. By June 1866 about 30,000 freedmen were working the land on these islands. Another successful all-black community was established at Mound Bayou, Mississippi, in 1867 by former slave Isaiah Thornton Montgomery. At the end of the war, President Johnson stated that the 'great plantations must be seized and divided into small portions, and sold to honest, industrious men'. This gave the impression that the Freedmen's Bureau would sell each freedman and loyal white 16 hectares (40 acres) from the available 324,000 hectares (800,000 acres) of abandoned or confiscated land, including 1,500 pieces of town property. In fact, the bureau was empowered only to rent out 16-hectare (40-acre) tracts – which were referred to as '40 acres and a mule' – to freedmen for three years, after which they might buy the land at slightly more than 16 times the yearly rent. Even if nothing else had intervened, few blacks could have bought the land at this price.

Inevitably, as ex-Confederates were pardoned by President Johnson, much of the confiscated land was returned to its former owners, causing severe disappointment to blacks who hoped to establish themselves as independent farmers. The most Congress would do was to pass the Southern Homestead Act of 1866, which made available an additional 17.4 million hectares (44 million acres) of Federal land in Alabama, Mississippi, Louisiana, Arkansas, and Florida to all settlers, regardless of 'race or color'.[8] Not only did this area contain poor soil, but few former slaves had the resources to survive even until their first harvest. Thus, although about four thousand blacks were resettled on homesteads under the new law, most were unable to establish farms. For example, in Georgia in 1876 blacks owned a mere 1.3 per cent of the total area.

In accordance with an Act of Congress passed on 25 July 1868, most of the operations of the Freedmen's Bureau were terminated on 31 December of that year. The exceptions were those of the Education Department, and the collection and payment of pensions to black war veterans. The former continued until 1872 and effected the most significant achievements of the bureau. Supported by

Northern freedmen's aid societies and black religious denominations, the bureau established free public schools for blacks and founded higher educational institutions such as Howard, Fisk, and Atlanta universities, plus the Hampton Institute.

The advocates of the Freedmen's Bureau had genuine intentions to help the African-American population prosper as free people. However, a lack of funding, insufficient support from the Federal government, weak internal organisation, opposition from conservatives, and the hostility of the Southern community ultimately tempered its success.

Sharecropping

The most common form of agriculture in the South after 1865 was sharecropping. The concept of sharecropping originated in the Black Codes, during the period of Presidential Reconstruction, as an attempt to limit black mobility and retain a 'captive' labour force. Under labour contracts issued, plantation owners provided freedmen with wages, housing, clothing, and food in return for fieldwork. Owing to a scarcity of cash, wages usually took the form of a very small share of the crop – often amounting to one-eighth or less, divided among the whole plantation's workforce. This system was actively encouraged by officials of the Freedmen's Bureau, who supported the Northern philosophy that wage earners could rise to the status of self-supporting tradesmen and property owners. Accordingly, bureau head Oliver O. Howard exhorted a group of Louisiana freedmen in 1865: 'You must begin at the bottom of the ladder and climb up.'

As a result, two main types of contractual arrangement developed within the share-tenancy system. Sharecroppers worked a plot belonging to their landlord in exchange for a house and a mule, plus tools, seed, and a share of the crop – usually between one-third and a half. Share-renters provided their own accommodation and farming supplies but paid a proportion of the crop, generally a third, as rent. At face value, this appeared to be a fair market compromise between the aspirations of freed slaves and land owners. In reality the system reduced blacks to a kind of neo-serfdom scarcely better than their former condition of slavery. Illiterate ex-slaves were cheated through one-sided contracts. They were forced to buy overpriced goods and provisions from plantation stores which, a few years before, had issued commissary goods within the slavery system. Combined with extortionate rates of interest, this often meant that by harvest time planters could claim 100 per cent or more of the annual crop. Disillusioned freedmen soon learned to chant the lament: 'Naught's a naught, and five's a figger/All for the white man, and none for the nigger.' Sharecropping continued in widespread use until the 1930s, but largely disappeared with the coming of farm mechanisation and a reduced need for cotton. Both factors resulted in fewer people working on the farms. There was no reason to employ so many workers any longer, and unemployment rates skyrocketed.

Black Reconstruction

During 1867 blacks and poor whites began to rebuild their state governments. They prepared new constitutions, approved the 14th and 15th Amendments, returned their states to the Union, and elected men to Congress. Consequently, blacks were voted into office, from state governor to local sheriff. With 76 of them among the 131 delegates, they played a decisive role in South Carolina's Constitutional Convention in 1868. Among the delegates were Robert B. Elliott and Francis L. Cardoza, both educated at British universities, and the Reverend Richard Cain, who declared: 'I want a constitution that shall do justice to all men. I have no prejudices and feel above making any distinctions.' The duly elected state government lowered the taxes on the poor, abolished imprisonment for debt, and granted voting rights to all, regardless of race or property. The state's first public-school system was established, and courts, county governments, hospitals, and prisons were built or reorganised. Congressman Joseph H. Rainey, a former slave who served two terms in the House of Representatives, declared with pride that the South Carolina constitution secured 'alike equal rights to all citizens, white and black, male and female, as far as possible. Mark you, we did not discriminate, although we had a majority.'

Great political changes took place throughout the Southern states. Northern writer Edward King toured the South in 1873. Like many Northerners, he had anti-black prejudices, but found the black contribution to government remarkable for a people recently released from slavery. In Virginia he visited a city council meeting and found it 'as well conducted as that of any Eastern city'. In Florida he discovered that the black state superintendent of education was a 'gentleman of considerable culture and capacity'. In Mississippi he observed blacks managing city affairs in 'a very satisfactory' manner.

Of the 22 black Congressmen who served their states from 1870 to 1901, half were college-educated men, and several held college degrees. Robert Smalls, who served five full terms as a South Carolina Congressman, was the Civil War hero who had delivered a Confederate gunboat to the Union Navy. Jefferson Long, the first black elected to the House of Representatives and Georgia's only black Congressman, had hid in a church belfry while seven of his supporters were shot in street fighting one election day. Later he became the first African American to make an official speech in the House, opposing leniency to former Confederates. These black statesmen were deeply concerned to protect the new rights of the freedmen. In the face of increasing segregation, they were the first blacks to battle for the passage of civil rights laws. But their various attempts to gain political and social equality met with diminishing success as the nineteenth century drew to a close. According to many Southern whites, the 'bottom rail was on top', and they did not intend to let it stay there long.

Reconstruction

2.1 Extracts from the Black Codes, approved in Mississippi on 25 November 1865

Section 1. Be it enacted . . . That all freedmen, free negroes, and mulattoes may sue and be sued, implead and be impleaded, in all the courts of law and equity of this State, and may acquire personal property, and choices in action, by descent or purchase, and may dispose of the same in the same manner and to the same extent that white persons may: Provided, That the provisions of this section shall not be so construed as to allow any freedman, free negro, or mulatto to rent or lease any lands or tenements except in incorporated cities or towns, in which places the corporate authorities shall control the same . . .

Section 3. . . . All freedmen, free negroes, or mulattoes who do now and have herebefore lived and cohabited together as husband and wife shall be taken and held in law as legally married, and the issue shall be taken and held as legitimate for all purposes; that it shall not be lawful for any freedman, free negro, or mulatto to intermarry with any white person; nor for any white person to intermarry with any freedman, free negro, or mulatto; and any person who shall so intermarry, shall be deemed guilty of felony, and on conviction thereof shall be confined in the State penitentiary for life; and those shall be deemed freedmen, free negroes, and mulattoes who are of pure negro blood, and those descended from a negro to the third generation, inclusive, though one ancestor in each generation may have been a white person.

Source: 'An Act to confer civil rights on freedmen, and for other purposes', *Mississippi, laws of the state . . .*, 1865 (Jackson, Mississippi, 1896), pp. 82–86

2.2 Telegram sent by General Phillip Sheridan to President Johnson, dated 6 August 1866, describing the New Orleans massacre

About 1 p.m. a procession of say from sixty to one hundred and thirty colored men marched up Burgundy street and crossed Canal street toward the Convention, carrying the American flag. These men had about one pistol to every ten men, and canes and clubs in addition. While crossing Canal street a row occurred. There were many spectators on the streets, and their manner and tone toward the procession [were] unfriendly. A shot was fired, by whom I am not able to state, but believe it to have been a policeman, or some colored man in the procession. This led to other shots, and a rush after the procession. On arrival at the front of the Institute there was some throwing of brickbats by both sides. The police, who had been well in hand, were vigorously marched to the scene of disorder. The procession entered the Institute with a flag, about six or eight remaining outside. A row occurred between a policeman and one of these colored men, and a shot was again fired by one of the parties, which led to an indiscriminate fire on the building through the windows by the policemen. This had been going on for a short time, when a white flag was displayed from the window of the

Institute, whereupon the firing ceased and the police rushed into the building. From the testimony of the wounded men and others who were inside the building, the police opened an indiscriminate fire upon the audience until they had emptied their revolvers, when they retired, and those inside barricaded the doors. The door was broken in and the firing again commenced, when many of the colored and white people either escaped through the door or were passed out by the policemen inside, but as they came out the policemen who formed the circle nearest the building fired upon them, and they again fired upon the citizens that formed the outer circle.

Many of those wounded and taken prisoner, and others who were prisoners and not wounded, were fired upon by their captors and by citizens. The wounded were stabbed while lying on the ground, and their heads beaten with brickbats. In the yard of the building, whither some of the colored men had escaped and partially secreted themselves, they were fired upon and killed or wounded by policemen. Some men were killed and wounded several squares from the scene.

Source: 'The New Orleans massacre', *Army & Navy Journal*, vol. 4, no. 2 (1 September 1866), p. 30

2.3 Circular no. 5 issued by the headquarters assistant commissioner, Bureau of Refugees, Freedmen and Abandoned Lands, South Carolina and Georgia, at Charleston, South Carolina, 19 October 1865

The impression prevails to a great extent among the freedmen that on the first of January 1866, the U.S. Government is to give them lands – homesteads of forty acres – and that for the coming year it is not necessary for them to contract with their former masters, or other employers for their labor. To correct this error, all Officers and Agents of the Bureau in South Carolina and Georgia, are hereby directed to give notice to the freedmen within their jurisdiction, that such expectations on their part are erroneous, and that the U.S. Government has no lands to divide among them.

Source: *Keowee Courier* (South Carolina), vol. 1, no. 9 (11 November 1865), p. 4

2.4 Extracts from the report of General James B. Steedman and General J. S. Fullerton, US Volunteers, who were ordered to tour the South to 'inspect and report upon the Freedmen's Bureau' during April 1866

In those districts of Virginia where the affairs of the Bureau have been faithfully and impartially administered by men of sound judgment and discretion, there has been no conflict between the agents of the Bureau and the citizens in the performance of their duties. But in many places, where the agents are not men of capacity and integrity, a very unsatisfactory condition of affairs exists . . .

Opposite Newbern [North Carolina], on the south bank of the Trent river, there is a settlement composed exclusively of freedmen, and containing a population of about four thousand, whose condition is truly deplorable. These unfortunate people came within our lines and were located there during the war. They are living in small huts, built by themselves, of lumber manufactured by hand. These huts generally contain but a single room, each of which is occupied, in most cases, by large families. The appearance of this settlement, recently scourged with small-pox, is well calculated to excite the deepest sympathy for the helpless condition of its inhabitants. The decrepid and helpless among them are supported by the Government of the United States, and the remainder procure an uncertain and scanty living from little jobs about Newbern, from fishing with small boats, etc. Rev. Mr. Fitz, formerly an army chaplain, presides over this colony, as 'Assistant Superintendent of the Bureau for the Trent River Settlement.' This agent has exercised the most arbitrary and despotic power, and practiced unheard of cruelties on the helpless freedmen under his charge. The outrageous conduct of this man was brought to our attention by a delegation of freedmen from the settlement, who called upon us and made statements in reference to his oppressions and outrages, which we could scarcely credit. After hearing these statements, we visited the settlement, conversed with the freedmen, investigated the charges against this man, and ascertained that he had been guilty of greater wrongs and oppressions than had been complained of. In addition to the testimony of the freedman, we took the statements of four intelligent ladies from the North, who were teaching school in this settlement.

Among the many acts of cruelty committed by Superintendent Fitz, we found that he had, in two instances, suspended freedmen with cords around their wrists, with their feet not touching the floor, and kept them in this position – in one case four and in the other case six hours. Also that he sentenced a freedman to an imprisonment of three months for a trivial offence – that of wrangling with his wife. He kept another man, who was arrested for debt, shut up in the block-house or prison for months, while his wife and children, reduced to abject destitution, died with the small-pox, and took him from the prison under guard, and compelled him to bury his lost child in the cradle in which it died.

Source: *Army & Navy Journal*, vol. 3, no. 39 (19 May 1866)

2.5 Extract from the report of the Freedmen's Bureau for 1869

At the close of the spring term there were known to be in the bureau 4,424 schools of all kinds, 9,503 teachers, and 256,353 pupils; and besides these a multitude of small schools scattered in rural byways of the South that are not included in this report, and not enrolled on the books of the Freedmen's Bureau. Seventeen of these schools, with 980 pupils, are industrial, teaching labor as well as knowledge. There are also 39 high and normal schools, with 3,377 pupils training to be teachers. Most of the scholars are teachers in small villages among the blacks during their long vacation. There are six colleges where a fair classical education can be obtained, and at Howard University [named after General O. O. Howard] there are between 50 and 100 scholars in the law, medical, and theological departments. Two hundred and ninety-two schools are entirely sustained by the freedmen, and 1,289 in part. Of the 250,000 pupils, over 192,000 were slaves before the war. About 759 school buildings are owned by the blacks themselves, while in Washington, Georgetown, Petersburg, Wilmington, and other places, the free-school system is fairly carried out to the blacks as well as the whites.

Source: *Army & Navy Journal*, vol. 7, no. 9 (16 October 1869)

2.6 Letter written by Brevet Captain C. M. Hamilton, US Army, describing how blacks in Marianna, Florida, met threats against their school and their white teacher

The night school has been frequently disturbed. One evening a mob called the teacher out of the school house, who on presenting himself was confronted with four revolvers, and menacing expressions of shooting him, if he did not promise to quit the place, and close the school. The freedmen promptly came to his aid, and the mob dispersed.

About the 18th or 19th of the month, I was absent . . . when quite a formidable disturbance took place at this school. The same mob threatened to destroy the School that night, and the freedmen learning this, assembled at their . . . place of instruction in a condition of self-defence.

I understand that not less than forty colored men armed to protect themselves, but the preparations becoming known to the respectable rowdies, they only maneuvered about in small squads, and were wise enough to avoid a collision.

It is to be lamented that such bitterness and anarchy should exist, and on my return I discountenanced the movement, even on the part of those who only sought self-protection. Yet I am gratified to report that the result of this affair has been quite salutary on the disposition of the people, for it seems to have infused a terror into them, and they now see the fearful necessity for law to rule, instead of mobs and riots.

Source: Office of the adjutant general, *Letters received*, vol. 4 (Washington DC: National Archives, War Records Office, 1866)

2.7 Edward King, a white Northerner who visited the South Carolina legislature in 1873, describes the changes taking place in Southern politics

The House, when I visited it, was composed of eighty-three colored members, all of whom are Republicans, and forty-one whites; the Senate consisted of fifteen colored men, ten white Republicans, and eight white Democrats. The President of the Senate and the Speaker of the House, both colored, were elegant and accomplished men, highly educated, who would have creditably presided over any commonwealth's [state's] legislative assembly . . . The little knot of white Democrats, massed together in one section of the hall, sat glum and scornful amid the mass of black speakers . . . There are men of real force and eloquence among the Negroes chosen to the House but they are the exception. In the Senate there was more decorum and ability among the members. Several of the colored senators spoke exceedingly well, and with great ease and grace of manner; others were awkward and lacked refinement . . .

I visited the University a day or two after the revolution caused there by the entrance of the first colored student, the Secretary of State himself. In the library . . . I saw the book from whose lists the white students had indignantly erased their names when they saw the Secretary's round, fair script beneath their own. The departure of the old professors and scholars was the signal for a grand onward movement by the blacks, and a great number entered the preparatory and law schools. They have summoned good teachers from the North, and are studying earnestly . . . While I was in the library a coal black senator arrived, with two members of the House, whom he presented to the head of the faculty as desirous of entering the law class. I was informed that dozens of members were occupied every spare moment outside of the sessions in faithful study.

Source: Edward King, 'The great South', *Scribner's Monthly*, vol. 8 (June 1874)

Document case-study questions

1 In what ways did the Black Codes enacted by Mississippi (Document 2.1) set out to limit the freedom of African-American people?

2 What impact might reports like that in Document 2.2 have on the success of Presidential Reconstruction?

3 How do you account for the fact that Document 2.3 had to be issued?

4 What conclusions can be drawn from Documents 2.4 and 2.5 regarding the work of the Freedmen's Bureau?

5 What can be learned of the experience of freedmen from Document 2.6?

6 To what extent does Document 2.7 illustrate the success of Black Reconstruction?

Notes and references

1 Hans L. Trefousse (ed.), *Background for Radical Reconstruction*, Boston: Little, Brown, 1970, p. 161.

2 'Report [of the] Select Committee on the Memphis Riot, July 25, 1866', *House reports*, 39th Congress, 2nd Session, vol. 3, no. 101, Washington: US Government Printing Office, 1866, p. 5.

3 'The New Orleans massacre', telegram from Sheridan to Grant, dated 2 August 1866, *Army & Navy Journal*, vol. 4, no. 2 (1 September 1866), p. 30.

4 Paul S. Boyer *et al.*, *The enduring vision: a history of the American people*, Lexington, Massachusetts: D. C. Heath & Company, 1996, p. 509.

5 *Army & Navy Journal*, vol. 2, no. 39 (20 May 1865), p. 619.

6 William Loren Katz, *Eyewitness: the negro in American history*, New York: Pittman Publishing Corporation, 1967, p. 241.

7 *Army & Navy Journal*, vol. 2, no. 50 (5 August 1865), p. 796.

8 'An Act for the disposal of public lands . . .' (21 June 1866), *US statutes at large, 39th Congress, 1st Session*, Boston: Little, Brown & Company, 1868, pp. 55–67.

3 Return of white supremacy

The Ku Klux Klan and other activists

Ku Klux Klan

With the election of Ulysses S. Grant to the presidency in 1868, the Republicans began slowly to disengage from Radical Reconstruction. Although not one of its architects, Grant did attempt to defend Reconstruction policies but, like millions of Americans, he had a belief in decentralised government and a reluctance to impose Federal authority on local and state affairs. Caught up in a number of scandals that involved his cabinet members, he had little time for the 'Southern question'.

Meanwhile, the Southern Democrats began a recovery. One mode of Democratic opposition to Reconstruction and civil rights took the form of secret societies. There were scores of such groups throughout the South, ranging from small bodies of neighbourhood police to great federated orders whose membership even extended into the Northern and western states. All of these orders opposed the freedman and his Republican support. The largest of them were the Ku Klux Klan (or the Invisible Empire), the Knights of the White Camellia, the Constitutional Union Guards, the Pale Faces, the White Brotherhood, the Council of Safety, and the '76 Association. By 1871 most of these orders had thrown off their disguise and appeared openly as armed whites fighting for control of Southern society.

The Ku Klux Klan was founded in a law office in Pulaski, Tennessee, during June 1866 by John Lester, James Crowe, John Kennedy, Calvin Jones, Richard Reed, and Frank McCord – six veterans of the Confederate Army who sought amusement after the excitement of wartime had given way to the tedium of civilian life. Influenced by the age of Greek classical learning, they chose the name 'Ku Klux', derived from the Greek word *kuklos*, meaning 'circle'. The word 'Klan' was presumably added because several of the originators came from Scottish or Irish stock.

Having begun with a strange name, it seemed natural for the founders of the Klan to adopt an organisation and ritual to match. The president was called the grand cyclops, and the vice-president was known as the grand magus. Other officers included the grand turk, or marshal; the grand exchequer, or treasurer; and two lictors or guardians of the den or meeting place. Lesser officers were called night hawks, goblins, furies, hydras, and genii. Ordinary members were called ghouls. The Klan members were required to maintain absolute secrecy regarding the organisation and its activities, and wore disguise when appearing in public to advertise their existence. Their original regalia usually consisted of a white mask with holes for eyes and nose, a tall conical cardboard hat, and a long flowing robe. When making public appearances, the original Klansmen communicated with each other by means of blasts on small whistles, using a code of signals.

Southern Democratic newspapers helped to popularise the movement by printing Klan advertisements, songs, jokes, and macabre warnings, plus favourable editorials. In Nashville, Ku Klux juvenile baseball teams were organised, and a music publisher brought out a song entitled the 'Kuklux midnight's roll call'. The name Ku Klux was applied as a brand name to knives, paint, and pills, and there was even 'Ku Klux Smoking Tobacco', containing the 'spirits of a hundred faithful K.K.K.'s' with an accurate and attractive full-length portrait of the 'Great Grand Cyclops' on the label.

The Ku Klux Klan quickly abandoned its social-club status. Following the passage of the Military Reconstruction Act in 1867, Klan leaders from all over Tennessee held a secret meeting in Nashville, and the 'hooded order' was transformed into a terrorist organisation. Nathan Bedford Forrest, an ex-Confederate general and outspoken critic of Republican Reconstruction, was elected grand wizard (president). The Ku Klux Klan spread rapidly throughout the rest of the South. By the end of 1867 the group claimed about 12,000 members in Alabama – about one in every nine white voters.

At first Klansmen hoped merely to frighten the freedmen and their white Republican supporters, and to discourage them from voting and holding public office. When this tactic failed, they turned to violence. According to historian Allen W. Trelease, by 1867 the Klan had become 'a counter-revolutionary device . . . For more than four years it whipped, shot, hanged, robbed, raped, and otherwise outraged Negroes and Republicans across the South in the name of preserving white civilization.'[1]

When freedmen 'made good money and had a good farm, the Ku Klux went to work and burned 'em down', recalled one black tenant farmer. In 1869 a Louisiana agent of the Freedmen's Bureau reported: 'Driving the freedmen from their crop and seizing it themselves when it is grown, is a complaint against the planters that comes to us from every quarter.'[2] Violence was equally felt in the cities. Richard Burke, a black Alabama lawyer, was killed for being too influential among 'people of his color'. Jack Dupree, a Republican leader in Mississippi, was murdered in front of his wife. When George Moore, an ex-slave in Alabama, voted Republican in the 1869 elections, Klan members beat him, raped a young girl visiting his wife, and attacked his neighbour.

In 1869 Nathan Bedford Forrest disbanded the Ku Klux Klan because of threats of governmental punishment. None the less, the majority of Klansmen refused to give up their terrorist activities, and increased their efforts after the elections of 1870. States such as Arkansas, Tennessee, and Texas enlisted an all-black state

Engraving of a Ku Klux Klan attack, published in *Harper's Weekly* on 24 February 1872. The original caption concluded: 'It is to be hoped that under a rigorous administration of the laws these deeds of violence will soon cease forever.'

militia to battle with the Klan, but their efforts only served to fan the flames. From the Southern white's point of view, a well-armed black militia was precisely what John Brown had sought to achieve at Harper's Ferry in 1859 when he led his attempted rebellion against slavery.

Nowhere did the Klan become more deeply entrenched than in the northern, or Piedmont, counties of South Carolina, where medium-sized farms predominated and the races were about equal in number. Possibly one of the largest Klan actions of the Reconstruction era took place in January 1871, when the Union county jail was assaulted by five hundred masked men. Eight black prisoners, accused of killing a Confederate veteran, were lynched. During the same period, hundreds of Republicans in Spartanburg, a largely white county with a Democratic majority, were whipped and saw their farm property destroyed. In York County nearly the entire white male population joined the Klan, committing at least 11 murders and hundreds of whippings.

One such incident occurred on the night of 6 March 1871, when James W. Avery and at least 40 other Klansmen attacked James Rainey, a Republican supporter and officer in the all-black state militia. After giving Rainey a brief, brutal beating, Klansmen dragged him to a nearby tree and lynched him. They then continued their rampage – beating and whipping black militiamen and their families. These acts of savagery echoed throughout the South as blacks and their white supporters reeled under a campaign of terror mounted by 'hooded riders' sworn to subvert the freedmen's newly won civil rights.

Ku-Klux Act, 1871

The South Carolina state courts were unwilling to prosecute members of the Ku Klux Klan. Attempts by the Republican governor Robert K. Scott to seek prosecutions for post-1870 election outrages proved unsuccessful. After concluding that the state's legal system was totally unable to protect blacks and prosecute Klansmen, a congressional investigation led by Attorney General Amos T. Ackerman recommended firmer action. Meanwhile, Congress passed the third Enforcement Act on 20 April 1871. Contemporaneously known as the Ku-Klux Act, this made it a felony for 'two or more persons' to conspire and go 'in disguise upon the public highway or upon the premises of another' for the purpose of depriving them of their civil rights and privileges. Those convicted of such crimes were to be punished with a maximum fine of $5,000 or by imprisonment, 'with or without hard labor, as the court may determine, for a period of not less than six months nor more than six years'.[3]

The Ku-Klux Act also empowered the president to use Federal troops to enforce the law and to suspend the writ of *habeas corpus* (the right to be brought before a judge and charged before being jailed for any length of time) in areas that he declared in insurrection. Thus in May 1871 President Grant ordered Major Lewis Merrill and a battalion of Federal troops to York County, the scene of some of the most brutal attacks. Merrill promptly began to make arrests, but local law-enforcement officials thwarted his efforts by handing the names of informers over to the Klan leadership.

On 12 October 1871 President Grant issued a proclamation ordering the Ku Klux Klan in South Carolina to disperse and surrender 'all arms, ammunition, uniforms, [and] disguises'.[4] Five days later, after little or no response, he showed one of the boldest displays of peacetime presidential power in US history by suspending the writ in nine South Carolina counties devastated by Klan attacks. About six hundred Klansmen were arrested by Major Merrill, and their trials began in Columbia, the state capital, on 28 November 1871. Federal prosecutors secured hundreds of convictions using predominantly black juries. Punishment consisted of fines or imprisonment, or both, depending on whether the accused had been a Klan leader. For example, Jonas Vassey, 'chief of the Horse Creek Klan', was fined $10 and jailed for one year, while John Burnett and David McLure were imprisoned for six and three months respectively.

After three main court sessions, the Ku Klux trials in South Carolina finally ran out of momentum during November 1872, with 1,188 cases still pending. Although similar trials began in other Southern states during the same year, by the summer of 1873 President Grant announced clemency for all Klansmen not yet tried. He also pardoned those who had been convicted and were still serving their sentence. Although the Ku Klux Klan had been destroyed as a public force, the 'hooded order' continued its illegal acts of terrorism, while other enemies of civil rights also began to emerge.

Battle of Liberty Place

The New Orleans Crescent City Democratic Club intimidated black voters in Louisiana during the 1868 and 1872 presidential elections. By 1874 this organisation was known as the White League and had grown to 14,000 members, who were dedicated to a 'white man's government' and the suppression of 'the insolent and barbarous African'. Emboldened by the liberal policies of Grant's administration in the wake of the Ku Klux Klan trials, and enraged by a disputed gubernatorial election, 3,500 armed White Leaguers assembled in New Orleans on 14 September 1874, demanding the resignation of the Republican governor, William Pitt Kellog.

Opposing the White League were 3,600 white policemen and black militia troops under the command of the ex-Confederate general James Longstreet. Supported by two Gatling guns and a battery of artillery, Longstreet's force formed a battle line in the streets of New Orleans, from Jackson Square to Canal Street, which protected the customs house in which the governor and other Republican officials had taken refuge. The White Leaguers charged the line, captured Longstreet, and pushed his men to the river, where they either surrendered or fled. The attackers occupied the city hall, statehouse, and arsenal. Total casualties in the one-hour struggle, known later as the Battle of Liberty Place, were 38 killed and 79 wounded.

The white supremacists deposed Kellog and installed the Democrat John McEnery as governor. He ran the state government of Louisiana for three days. Meanwhile, President Grant ordered Federal troops to New Orleans. Upon their arrival, the White Leaguers withdrew, William Kellog was reinstated as governor, and Longstreet was released. None the less, the Battle of Liberty Place was a pivotal event which sent ripples throughout the South, and it helped the Democrats to win major gains at the polls in 1874 – signalling the beginning of the end of Reconstruction.

Mississippi Plan

A systematic campaign of physical threats and blatant violence against black and white Republican voters enabled white supremacists to take over the government of Mississippi illegally in 1875. As chairman of the Democratic State Executive Committee, James Zachariah George was the chief architect of the 'Mississippi Plan'. White Democrats and veterans of the Confederate Army formed themselves into paramilitary organisations thinly disguised as either 'rifle clubs' or mounted 'sabre clubs' – in theory dependent on whether they had served as infantry or cavalry during the Civil War. First organised in Mississippi, these groups wore red shirts to show their defiance of the Republican Scalawags and Carpetbaggers. Illegally armed with 'rifles and pistols and such other arms as they may command', the Red Shirts did their utmost to intimidate black voters and white Republicans.

Seventy-five blacks were killed in Vicksburg, Mississippi, during 'race riots' stirred up by the Red Shirts on 7 December 1874. Two weeks later, Federal troops again restored calm and dispersed 'disorderly gatherings'. Further 'riots' occurred during July and September 1875 and finally, during the presidential election of 2 November 1875, the Red Shirts applied so much 'force, fraud, or intimidation' that the Democrats won control of the state of Mississippi. As a result Mississippi became the only state with a black majority to be seized by an anti-Reconstruction Democratic administration during Grant's two terms in office.

In 1876 the same tactics were employed in the three remaining Southern Republican states. Despite again being ordered to disperse in October 1876, the Red Shirts in South Carolina helped elect Wade Hampton III, an ex-Confederate general, as governor, and returned the Democratic Party to power in that state. Similar violence and intimidation in Louisiana and Florida also established Democratic governments and solidified the South as a virtual one-party system for decades to come.

Reconstruction ends

The demise of Reconstruction was also hastened by a split in the Republican Party during 1872. Among other things, the Liberal Republicans condemned the Radicals for their 'bayonet rule' in the South. Optimistically, they claimed that Reconstruction had achieved its goal, and that blacks could manage for themselves now they had been enfranchised. With the resurgence of the Southern Democratic Party, and a steady reduction of troop levels, only three Southern states – South Carolina, Florida, and Louisiana – had Reconstruction governments by 1876.

The fate of the freedman was finally sealed as part of the political 'deal' that gave the 1876 presidential election to the Republican Rutherford B. Hayes. When it first became apparent that he had lost to Democrat Samuel Tilden, Hayes announced: 'I don't care for myself; and the [Republican] party . . . and the country, too, can stand it; but I do care for the poor colored man of the South.' But several weeks later he declared that he was convinced that 'absolute justice and fair play' could be best achieved by the blacks by 'trusting the honorable and influential whites'.

To solve an indecisive presidential election result, the two political parties exchanged promises that if Hayes could move into the White House Federal troops would be removed from South Carolina and Louisiana, and the Democrats could gain control of those states. Once in office, Hayes fulfilled his part of the bargain. During April 1877 he ordered Federal soldiers guarding the South Carolina and Louisiana statehouses back to their barracks. However, on Hayes's Inauguration Day on 5 March 1877 whites in Hamburg, South Carolina, had attacked and killed scores of local black citizens. Without protection from a large military presence, black civil rights in the South came under serious threat of extinction, and subsequent decades would see a new era of disenfranchisement, segregation, and terror.

The end of Reconstruction in 1877 was accompanied by the collapse of the Republican Party in the South, and the advent of the so-called period of Redemption, during which the white supremacists repudiated equal rights for black people. This return to power of a Southern white elite, known as the 'Redeemers', had disastrous results for American blacks. An agrarian faction within their number, called the Bourbons (after the French royal house recalled after Napoleon Bonaparte's downfall), represented the old pre-Civil War planter aristocracy. Although divided on many issues, all Redeemers shared two common goals – to oust the Republicans and to deny blacks their recently won civil rights.

Lynching

The term 'lynch' originated in western Virginia, deriving from the activities of Colonel Charles Lynch. A colonel during the Revolutionary War, 'Judge' Lynch presided over an illegal court that hanged 'Tories', or colonists who remained loyal to the Crown, without the right to trial. This arbitrary form of justice became known as lynch law, and was used to describe the hanging of mostly black people by white mobs in the South during the post-Reconstruction period.

Sources vary regarding the gruesome toll of murder by lynching committed in the name of justice. A study by Tolnay and Beck published in 1992 documented 2,805 victims of lynch mobs killed between 1882 and 1930 in ten Southern states. Of this number, about 2,500 were African Americans while the remainder were white people. The scale of this carnage means that, on the average, one black man, woman, or child was murdered every week between 1882 and 1930.[5] Meanwhile, in the west, which was predominantly white, 38 blacks and 447 whites were the victims of lynching during the same period. The worst year throughout the whole of the United States was 1892, when at least 235 African Americans were lynched by hate-driven white mobs.

By the end of the nineteenth century, lynching mostly occurred in the Deep South – Mississippi, Alabama, Louisiana and Georgia – and was almost exclusively racially motivated. The most frequent cause of lynching was suspected murder, theft, or damage to property – although racists tried to maintain the idea that the main cause was rape or attempted rape. In fact, only about one-sixth of lynchings were prompted by rape allegations. Lynching was often preceded by a 'trial' during which the victims were tied up and beaten into making a 'confession'. They were frequently burned, tortured, or shot before finally being hanged.

Response of the African Americans

Exodusters

As the last Federal troops left the South in 1877, and Reconstruction gave way to renewed racial oppression, thousands of blacks decided to leave the South. Some, like Henry McNeal Turner, one of the first bishops in the African-American

Episcopal Church, encouraged a return to Africa, but most were reluctant to leave the country that represented the only home they knew.

Benjamin 'Pap' Singleton was born a slave in Davidson County, Tennessee, but escaped to Canada and lived there until the Emancipation Proclamation came into effect in January 1863. Returning to Tennessee after the Union occupation, he earned a living making coffins. By the late 1860s a number of factors – including impoverished conditions, recent outbreaks of racial violence by whites, and a Democratic Party victory in the 1869 elections – combined to cause discontent among the freedmen of Nashville. In response Singleton formed the Tennessee Real Estate and Homestead Association, which was meant to assist blacks in acquiring land to settle on in the South. When this attempt proved unsuccessful, he urged blacks to form their own independent communities in north-western Kansas, which at the time was trying to attract settlers, both black and white. But for African Americans there was an additional attraction. Their memories of slavery were still vivid, and the story of abolitionist John Brown's efforts to prevent the spread westwards of 'the peculiar institution' during the 1850s gave a special quality to Kansas in the eyes of blacks in the Deep South. Because they believed they would find their promised land in the west, those who followed Singleton's advice later became known as the 'Exodusters', after the Exodus or escape of the Israelites from Egypt in biblical times.

By 1875 Singleton and associates had founded the Edgefield Real Estate Association, which held rallies, raised funds, and published newspapers to promote black migration. They also issued handbills declaring: 'Ho for Kansas!', and spread circulars entitled 'The advantage of living in a free state'. Distributed throughout the cotton states, by 1879 these had encouraged approximately 20,000 blacks to emigrate to Kansas, mostly from Louisiana, Mississippi, and Texas.

The industry of these black pioneers brought approving notices in Kansas newspapers. One story concerned a farmer who with one cow 'broke and improved 12 acres [4.9 hectares] of prairie and cultivated 8 acres [3.2 hectares] of corn; his wife drives the cow and keeps the flies off'. Another planted a 4-foot (1.2-metre) hedgerow around 160 acres (65 hectares) of land.

The movement continued into 1880, when a further 60,000 Exodusters gathered at Nashville to begin the journey to a new life. They travelled by rail; by steamboat up the Mississippi and Missouri rivers; and over land by wagon, mule, or on foot. Arriving in the 'promised land', they swelled the population of Kansas communities such as Atchison, Wyandotte (present-day Kansas City), and Topeka, or established all-black townships like Hill City, Wildhorse, and Nicodemus. Promoted as the 'largest colored colony in America', Nicodemus was founded in September 1877 when a white promoter called W. R. Hill guided 30 black settlers to the Solomon Valley. By 1880 Nicodemus was home to 260 black residents.

At first, Kansans welcomed the Exodusters, but before long the governor and railroad officials tried to discourage further black migration. Circulars and handbills were sent out saying that all the good land was taken, that no labourers were needed, and that each family would need $500 with which to settle. Not only did the migration of black people stop, but two-thirds left the state. The towns began to disappear as the Exodusters died, returned to the South, or moved on to other opportunities in the west.

This black exodus was criticised as a 'foolish project' in the Tennessee press, and white employers supported a campaign to attract Chinese labourers to replace the black workers. Frederick Douglass and other Republicans also opposed the movement, claiming that blacks should remain in the South to fight for their civil rights. Booker T. Washington urged those considering emigration to 'cast their bucket down' where they were.

Benjamin 'Pap' Singleton responded by declaring, 'Such men as this should not be leaders of our race any longer.' In 1880 he claimed in testimony before a US committee to be 'the whole cause of the Kansas immigration'. A congressional investigation attempted to halt the exodus during the following year. Although Ben Singleton died in Kansas during the late 1880s and was buried in an unmarked grave, the movement continued unabated as others established politically independent and economically viable all-black communities in Oklahoma, Texas, Iowa, New Mexico, and California.

Return of white supremacy

3.1 Report published in the *Planter's Banner* of Louisiana on 23 May 1868; an example of the manner in which the Klan was reported by the Southern newspapers

There is much excitement among the negroes and even some of the white folks, all over Attakapas, about the Ku-Kluxes that have lately appeared in this country. I am not superstitious, and will not tell you what I believe about these strange, ghostly appearances, but will give you some general items and rumors.

The negroes have entirely deserted one prairie in Attakapas since the election, having been run out by the Ku Kluxes.

The negroes of Lafayette parish were lately nearly all of them preparing to leave, the K.K.K.'s having frightened them every night, and carried off a carpet-bagger from Illinois. One negro, a big-talking radical, somewhere in the parish of St. Martin, was lately carried off by these confederate ghosts, at night, and has never been heard of since.

A night traveller called at the negro quarters, somewhere in Attakapas, and asked for water. After he had drunk three blue buckets full of good cistern water, at which the negro was much astonished, he thanked the colored man and told him he was very thirsty, that he had travelled nearly a thousand miles in twenty-four hours, and that was the best drink of water he had since he was killed at the battle of Shiloh [1862]. The negro dropped the bucket, tumbled over two chairs and a table, escaped through a back window, and has not since been heard from. He was a radical negro.

White men on white horses have lately been seen sailing through the air at midnight at Pattersonville, Jeanerette, and at various places all over the southern part of this State.

If negroes attempt to run away from the K.K.K.'s, these spirits always follow them, and catch them, and no living man hears from them again.

The leader of this new order is said to be perfectly terrible. He is ten feet [3 metres] high and his horse is fifteen [4.6 metres]. He carries a lance and a shield like those of Goliath of the Philistines . . .

Attakapas, May 20, 1868.   K.K.K.

Source: Walter L. Fleming (ed.), *Documentary history of Reconstruction: political, military, social, religious, educational and industrial, 1865 to 1906*, vol. 1 (1906), p. 365

3.2 Account of a Ku Klux Klan parade in Pulaski, Tennessee

On the morning of the 4th of July, 1867, the citizens of Pulaski found the sidewalks thickly strewn with slips of paper bearing the printed words: 'The Ku Klux will parade the streets tonight.' This announcement created great excitement. The people supposed that their curiosity, so long baffled, would now be gratified. They were confident that this parade would at least afford them the opportunity to find out who were the Ku Klux.

Soon after nightfall the streets were lined with an expectant and excited throng of people . . . The members of the Klan in the country left their homes in the afternoon and traveled alone or in squads of two or three, with their paraphernalia carefully concealed . . . After nightfall they assembled at designated points near the four main roads leading into town. Here they donned their robes and disguises and put covers of gaudy materials on their horses. A sky-rocket sent up from some point in the town was the signal to mount and move. The different companies met and passed each other on the public square in perfect silence; the discipline appeared to be admirable. Not a word was spoken. Necessary orders were given by means of the whistles. In single file, in death-like stillness, with funeral slowness, they marched and counter-marched throughout the town. While the column was headed North on one street it was going South on another. By crossing over in opposite directions the lines were kept up in almost unbroken continuity. The effect was to create the impression of vast numbers. This marching and counter-marching was kept up for about two hours, and the Klan departed as noiselessly as they came . . .

This demonstration had the effect for which it was designated. Perhaps the greatest illusion produced by it was in regard to the numbers participating in it . . . [Some] were confident that the number was not less than three thousand. Others, whose imaginations were more easily wrought upon, were quite certain there were ten thousand. The truth is, that the number of Ku Klux in the parade did not exceed four hundred. This delusion in regard to numbers prevailed wherever the Ku Klux appeared . . .

Source: Fleming (ed.), *Documentary history of Reconstruction*, vol. 1, pp. 367–68

3.3 Notice posted in Union, South Carolina, March 1871

K.K.K.

Headquarters, Ninth division, S.C.

Special Orders No. 3, K.K.K.

'Ignorance is the curse of God.'

For this reason, we are determined that members of the Legislature, the School Commissioner and County Commissioners of Union, shall no longer officiate.

Fifteen (15) days' notice from this date, is therefore given, and if they, *one and all*, do not *at once and forever resign* their present inhuman, disgraceful and outrageous rule, then retributive justice will surely be used as night follows day.

Also—An honest man is the noblest work of God.

For this reason, if the Clerk of the said Board of County Commissioners and School Commissioners does not immediately renounce and relinquish his present position, then harsher measures than this will most assuredly and certainly be used . . .

By order Grand Chief.

A.O., Grand Secretary.

March 9, A.D. 1871.

Source: *Keowee Courier* (South Carolina), vol. 6, no. 22 (24 March 1871), p. 2

3.4 Report on the Ku Klux Klan trials published in January 1872

Mr. Corbin called John Harris, one of the colored men whipped, who gave a description of his being whipped in a severe manner by the Ku-Klux.

Munroe Scruggs was called up, and asked what he had to say in extenuation of his offence. He stated that he had been . . . forced into the order. Judge Bryan stated to him, that on account of his youth, the court was inclined to deal as leniently with him as possible; and after characterizing the outrages committed as unmanly and unbecoming a true son of South Carolina, and calculated to bring shame on her fair name, sentenced him to pay a fine of $10 and be imprisoned for six months . . .

Wm. Self, who stated that he had been on three raids; whipped three negroes—two women and one man—on the first raid; there was nothing said about politics. On the second, a man named Roberts was ordered to stop selling whiskey near a church, on church days; and the third was to take a colored man back to his wife, whom he had left . . . Junius B. Tindall, who stated that he had been on one raid, when a man and woman had been made to thrash one another for illicit cohabitation, and on another raid, to disperse a crowd of negroes frolicking on a widow's place contrary to her wishes, was sentenced to one year's imprisonment . . .

Calvin Cook stated that he had been on but one raid, against James Lawrence, a white man; and, as the witness thought, a Democrat. He was whipped because he was suspected of concealing stolen money. Cook was sentenced to three months' imprisonment.

Source: *Keowee Courier*, vol. 7, no. 11 (12 January 1872), p. 2

3.5 Cartoon by Thomas Nast

Published on 24 October 1874, this *Harper's Weekly* engraving by Thomas Nast entitled 'Worse Than Slavery' was a commentary on the growing power of white supremacy during the Reconstruction period.

Source: *Harper's Weekly*, 1874

3.6 Excerpts from the instructions to Red Shirts in South Carolina, 1876

1. That every Democrat in the Townships must be put upon the Roll of the Democratic Clubs . . .

2. That a Roster must be made of every white and of every Negro in the Townships and returned immediately to the County Executive Committee.

3. That the Democratic Military Clubs are to be armed with rifles and pistols and such other arms as they may command. They are to be divided into two companies, one of the old men, the other of the young men; an experienced captain or commander to be placed over each of them . . .

12. Every Democrat must feel honor bound to control the vote of at least one Negro, by intimidation, purchase, keeping him away or as each individual may determine, how he may best accomplish it.

13. We must attend every Radical meeting that we hear of whether they meet at night or in the day time. Democrats must go in as large numbers as they can get together, and well armed, behave at first with great courtesy and assure the ignorant Negroes that you mean them no harm and so soon as their leaders or speakers begin to speak and make false statements of the facts, tell them then and there to their faces, that they are liars, thieves and rascals, and are only trying to mislead the ignorant Negroes and if you get a chance get upon the platform and address the Negroes.

14. In speeches to Negroes you must remember that argument has no effect upon them; they can only be influenced by their fears, superstitions and cupidity. Do not attempt to flatter and persuade them . . . Treat them so as to show them, you are the superior race, and that their natural position is that of subordination to the white man . . .

16. Never threaten a man individually. If he deserves to be threatened, the necessities of the times require that he should die . . .

29. Every club must be uniformed in a red shirt and they must be sure and wear it upon all public meetings and particularly on the day of election.

30. Secrecy should shroud all of our transactions. Let not your left hand know what your right hand does.

Source: William A. Sheppard (ed.), *Red Shirts remembered: Southern brigadiers of the Reconstruction period*, Atlanta, Georgia: Ruralist Press, 1940, pp. 46–50

3.7 Findings of the inquiry into how far the rights of the people of Mississippi were violated by 'force, fraud, or intimidation' at the election held on 2 November 1875

(1.) The committee find that the young men of the State, especially those who reached manhood during the war, or who have arrived at that condition since the war, constitute the nucleus and the main force of the dangerous element.

As far as the testimony taken by the committee throws any light upon the subject, it tends, however, to establish the fact that the democratic organizations, both in the counties and in the State, encouraged the young men in their course, accepted the political advantages of their conduct, and are in a large degree responsible for the criminal results.

(2.) There was a general disposition on the part of white employers to compel the laborers to vote the democratic ticket. This disposition was made manifest by newspaper articles, by the resolutions of conventions, and by the declarations of landowners, planters, and farmers to the workmen whom they employed, and by the incorporation in contracts of a provision that they should be void in case the negroes voted the republican ticket.

(3.) Democratic clubs were organized in all parts of the State, and the able-bodied members were also organized generally into military companies and furnished with the best arms that could be procured in the country. The fact of their existence was no secret, although persons not in sympathy with the movement were excluded from membership. Indeed their object was more fully attained by public declarations of their organization in connection with the intention, everywhere expressed, that it was their purpose to carry the election at all hazards.

In many places these organizations possessed one or more pieces of artillery. These pieces of artillery were carried over the counties and discharged upon the roads in the neighborhood of republican meetings, and at meetings held by the democrats. For many weeks before the election members of this military organization traversed the various counties, menacing the voters and discharging their guns by night as well as by day . . .

(4.) It appears from testimony that, for some time previous to the election, it was impossible, in a large number of the counties, to hold republican meetings. In the republican counties of Warren, Hinds, Lowndes, Monroe, Copiah, and Holmes meetings of the republicans were disturbed or broken up, and all attempts to engage in public discussion were abandoned by the republicans many weeks before the election.

(5.) The riots of Vicksburgh [*sic*] on the 5th of July, and at Clinton on the 4th of September, were the results of a special purpose on the part of the democrats to break up the meetings of the republicans, to destroy the leaders, and to inaugurate an era of terror, not only in those counties, but throughout the State, which would deter republicans, and particularly the negroes, from organizing or attending meetings, and especially deter them from the free exercise of the right to vote on the day of the election. The results sought for were in a large degree attained . . .

(15.) The committee find that if in the counties named there had been a free election, republican candidates would have been chosen, and the character of the legislature so changed that there would have been 66 republicans to 50 democrats in the house, and 26 republicans to 11 democrats in the senate; and that consequently the present legislature of Mississippi is not a legal body, and that its acts are not entitled to recognition by the political department of the Government of the United States, although the President may, in his discretion, recognize it as a government de facto for the preservation of the public peace.

Source: *Mississippi in 1875: report of the select committee to inquire into the Mississippi election of 1875 . . .*, Senate reports, no. 527 (44th Congress, 1st Session), III, pp. ix–xxxix, reprinted in Robert W. Johannsen, *Reconstruction, 1865–1877*, New York: Free Press, 1970, pp. 173–82

3.8 Press report of a lynching

NEGRO IS LYNCHED AT GARLAND CITY

Brutally attacked a White Man Saturday

Special to the Gazette, Garland City, July 30. Andrew Avery the Negro who shot and fatally wounded Will Woods, a white man, near here Saturday morning, was hanged by a mob in the heart of town tonight at 9:45. About 40 men were in the party. The Lynching was conducted in a quiet fashion.

Source: *Arkansas Gazette*, 31 July 1917

3.9 Handbill produced by the Nicodemus Town Company to encourage blacks to settle in Kansas

To the Colored Citizens of the United States

Nicodemus, Graham Co., Kan., July 2d. 1877

We, the Nicodemus Town Company of Graham County, Kan., are now in possession of our lands and the Town Site of Nicodemus, which is beautifully located on the N. W. quarter of Section I Town 8, Range 21 in Graham Co., Kansas, in the great Solomon Valley, 240 miles west of Topeka, and we are proud to say it is the finest country we ever saw. The soil is of a rich, black, sandy loam. The country is rather rolling, and looks most pleasing to the human eye. The south fork of the Solomon river flows through Graham County, nearly directly east and west and has an abundance of excellent water, while there are numerous springs of living water abounding throughout the Valley. There is an abundance of fine Magnesian stone for building purposes, which is much easier handled than the rough sand or hard stone. There is also some timber; plenty for fire use, while we have no fear but what we will find plenty of coal.

Now is your time to secure your home on Government Land in the Great Solomon Valley of Western Kansas.

Remember, we have secured the service of W. R. Hill, a man of energy and ability, to locate our Colony.

Not quite 90 days ago we secured our charter for locating the town site of Nicodemus. We then became an organized body with only three dollars in the treasury and twelve members, but under the careful management of our officers, we have now nearly 300 good and reliable members, with several members permanently located on their claims—with plenty of provisions for the colony—while we are daily receiving letters from all parts of the country from parties desiring to locate in the great Solomon Valley of Western Kansas.

For Maps, Circulars, and Passenger rates, address our General Manager, W. R. HILL, North Topeka, Kansas, until August 1st, 1877, then at Hill City, Graham Co., via Trego.

Rev. S. P. ROUNDTREE, Sec'y

Source: Kansas Historical Society

3.10 Eyewitness description of the arrival of the first Exodusters at Wyandotte, Kansas, in 1879

One morning in April, 1879, a Missouri steamboat arrived at Wyandotte, Kansas, and discharged a load of colored men, women and children, with divers barrels, boxes, and bundles of household effects. It was a novel, picturesque, pathetic sight. They were of all ages and sizes . . . their garments were incredibly patched and tattered, stretched, and uncertain . . . and there was not probably a dollar in money in the pockets of the entire party. The wind was eager, and they stood upon the wharf shivering . . . They looked like persons coming out of a dream. And indeed, such they were . . . for this was the advance guard of the Exodus.

Soon other and similar parties came by the same route, and still others, until, within a fortnight, a thousand or more of them were gathered there at the gateway of Kansas— all poor, some sick, and none with a plan of future action . . .

The case was one to appeal with force to popular sympathy . . . So temporary shelter was speedily provided for them; food and facilities for cooking it were furnished them in ample measure . . . Then came more of them. The tide swelled daily . . .

The closing autumn found at least 15,000 of these colored immigrants in Kansas. Such of them as had arrived early in the spring had been enabled to do something toward getting a start, and the thriftier and more capable ones had made homestead-entries and contrived, with timely-aid, to build cabins; in some cases, small crops of corn and garden vegetables were raised . . .

Numerous cabins of stone and sod were constructed while the cold season lasted . . . in many cases, the women went to the towns and took in washing, or worked as house-servants . . . while the men were doing the building. Those who could find employment on the farms about their 'claims', worked willingly and for small wages, and in this way supported their families, and procured now and then a calf, a pig, or a little poultry; others obtained places on the railroads, in the coal-mines, and on the public works at Topeka. Such as got work at any price, did not ask assistance; those who were compelled to apply for aid did it slowly, as a rule, and rarely came a second time. Not a single colored tramp was seen in Kansas all winter; and only one colored person was convicted of any crime . . .

. . . their savings are not remarkable, to be sure, but they are creditable, and not to be lightly passed over. The wonder is that they have anything whatever to show for . . . twelve months of hand-to-mouth hardship and embarrassment.

Source: Henry King, 'A year of the exodus in Kansas', *Scribner's Monthly*, vol. 8 (June 1880), pp. 211–15

Document case-study questions

1 With reference to Documents 3.1, 3.2, and 3.3, identify the main methods of intimidation used by the Ku Klux Klan.

2 What conclusions can be drawn from Document 3.4 regarding attempts to control white racism?

3 What point is Document 3.5 making about white supremacists?

4 How useful are Documents 3.6 and 3.7 for a historian constructing a history of Southern white racism during the Reconstruction period?

5 What can be learned from Document 3.8 about attitudes towards lynching?

6 What concerns that blacks might have had about going west to Kansas are evident from a comparison of Document 3.9 and Document 3.10?

Notes and references

1 Allen W. Trelease, *White terror: the Ku Klux Klan conspiracy and Southern Reconstruction*, Westport, Connecticut: Greenwood Press, 1971, p. xi.

2 William Loren Katz, *Eyewitness: the negro in American history*, New York: Pittman Publishing Corporation, 1967, pp. 266–67.

3 *Keowee Courier* (South Carolina), vol. 6, no. 28 (6 May 1871), p. 1.

4 'Proclamation by the president', *Keowee Courier*, vol. 7, no. 1 (27 October 1871), p. 1.

5 Stewart E. Tolnay and E. M. Beck, *A festival of violence: an analysis of Southern lynchings, 1882–1930*, Urbana and Chicago: University of Illinois Press, 1992, p. ix.

4 Jim Crow

Decline in the rights of the African American

The 'Jim Crow' laws, passed during the late nineteenth century by the Southern states of America for the purpose of segregating blacks from whites, were named after a song called 'Jump Jim Crow', composed in 1828 by a minstrel-show performer called Thomas Dartmouth 'Daddy' Rice. The minstrel show was one of the first indigenous forms of white American entertainment, sometimes involving white men blacking their faces and performing song-and-dance routines on stage which mimicked or made fun of black people. Thomas Rice, a white actor, was inspired by an elderly black in Louisville, Kentucky, who danced and sang to a song that ended with the chorus: 'Wheel about and turn about and do jis so/Eb'ry time I wheel about I jump Jim Crow.' Rice's stage act appealed to white prejudice, both Northern and Southern, and took him from Louisville to Cincinnati, from Pittsburgh to Philadelphia, and finally to New York City in 1832.

Representing a revival of an aspect of the pre-Civil War belief in states' rights, the Jim Crow laws deprived blacks of their hard-earned civil rights and created a racial caste system that was to last until the 1950s.

Supreme Court v. civil rights

In the years following the Civil War, the supporters of civil rights experienced opposition from an unexpected quarter. As early as 1866 the findings of the US Supreme Court in the case called *Ex parte Milligan* inadvertently deprived the freedman of fundamental civil rights by denying him access to the law. In 1864 a civilian anti-war Democrat called Lambdin P. Milligan had been sentenced to death by an army court in Indiana for disloyal activities. Abraham Lincoln delayed his execution, but after the president's assassination Andrew Johnson approved the sentence. Milligan's attorney appealed for his release under the Habeas Corpus Act of 1863, but the Federal circuit court was divided on the question of whether civilian courts had jurisdiction over appeals from military tribunals. When the matter was referred to the Supreme Court, Associate Judge David Davis ruled that a military commission established by the president or Congress could not try civilians in areas remote from war where civil courts were functioning. Although this was considered an extremely important Supreme Court decision which upheld the civil rights of all white Americans, the special military courts established to enforce the Supplementary Freedmen's Bureau Act of 1866 in defence of blacks were quickly rendered powerless. Hence, the newly freed African Americans lost a major source of support.

During the Slaughterhouse cases of 1873, the Supreme Court further weakened the position of blacks. Although concerned with a business monopoly rather than civil rights, these cases provided the opponents of Reconstruction with an opportunity to offer a narrow interpretation of the 14th Amendment. In 1869 the Louisiana legislature had granted a 25-year monopoly over the New Orleans slaughterhouse trade to one firm, the Crescent City Livestock Landing and Slaughterhouse Company, and had closed down all other slaughterhouses in the interests of public health. The excluded butchers claimed they had been deprived of their lawful occupation 'without due process of law', and argued that such action violated the 14th Amendment, which guaranteed state legislature could not 'abridge the privileges or immunities' of US citizens.

The Supreme Court upheld the Louisiana legislature by issuing a doctrine of 'dual citizenship'. This maintained that the 14th Amendment protected only the rights of national citizenship – for example the right of interstate travel, or the entitlement to Federal protection when abroad on the high seas. It did not protect the basic civil rights bestowed on citizens by virtue of their state citizenship. The decision in the Slaughterhouse cases came close to destroying the 14th Amendment, and freedmen found their civil rights under threat as white supremacists took control of Southern state legislatures.

However, the Supreme Court again backed away from Reconstruction in 1875, with regard to voting rights bestowed via the 15th Amendment. In the case of US v. Reese, the court ruled in favour of Kentucky officials who were charged with turning away would-be black voters. Declaring parts of the first Enforcement Act unconstitutional, the judges held that the 15th Amendment did not guarantee the right to vote, and that states alone could confer voting rights on individuals. As a result of US v. Cruikshank in 1876, the Supreme Court dismissed indictments against nine members of the Ku Klux Klan who attacked a political gathering of black citizens in Colfax Parish, Louisiana, killing or wounding more than a hundred African Americans. The court ruled that the 14th Amendment protected the rights and privileges of citizens only when they were infringed by the action of a state. Hence racial crimes perpetuated by individuals were not the target of Federal law.

By the 1880s the judicial retreat from civil rights was in full swing. In a group of cases referred to during 1883 as the 'civil rights cases', the Supreme Court ruled that the Civil Rights Act of 1875, which forbade racial discrimination in public places, was unconstitutional. The court also ruled that the 14th Amendment prohibited state governments from discriminating against people because of race but did not restrict private organisations or individuals from doing so. Thus railroads, hotels, and theatres could legally practise segregation. Summing up, Judge Joseph P. Bradley of New York declared that the black man must cease 'to be the special favorite of the laws', and must seek protection for his rights 'in the ordinary modes by which other men's rights are protected'. The civil rights cases did much to pave the way to social segregation and 'Jim Crow'.

Plessy v. Ferguson

Railroads were quick to deny blacks entrance to regular passenger cars or carriages. African Americans travelling by rail were confined to so-called 'Jim Crow' cars, which were set aside exclusively for blacks. The first law requiring separate accommodation for the races on board trains was passed in Louisiana in 1878. Seven other Southern states had followed suit by 1891. The passage of the Separate Car Act in Louisiana during 1890 enraged two New Orleans groups dedicated to assuring fair treatment for African Americans and mulattoes. One of these groups was represented by *The Crusader*, a weekly black newspaper founded in 1889 by the New Orleans attorney Louis Martinet. Through one of its columnists, Rodolphe Desdunes, this journal severely attacked the new Act. The other New Orleans group was the Comité des Citoyens, or Citizens' Committee, formed in 1890 to fight legal battles against discrimination. These two groups joined forces, and set about raising funds from benevolent, social, and religious organisations throughout the United States. Their ultimate goal was to see the Louisiana Jim Crow law struck down in the courts – and a New Orleans shoemaker of mulatto origin called Homer Plessy would be their means of doing so.

Homer Plessy became the focal point of a carefully orchestrated act of civil disobedience that took place almost 70 years before the twentieth-century civil rights movement began.[1] A French-speaking Roman Catholic, he possessed fair skin which made him appear almost white. On 7 June 1892 Plessy bought a first-class ticket at the Press Street depot in New Orleans, to travel on an East Louisiana Railroad passenger train destined for Covington, Louisiana. Shortly before departure, he sat down in a day coach designated for white passengers only. After the train had left the station, Conductor J. J. Dowling confronted Plessy, and asked if he was a 'colored' man. Plessy answered in the affirmative and refused to leave the car. The train was stopped and he was taken to the Fifth Street police station, where he was booked and released on temporary bail set by a judge. The *Plessy v. Ferguson* case had begun.

Although Homer Plessy's sponsors initially felt certain they would win the ensuing court case, they found themselves appealing to John Howard Ferguson, a 54-year-old judge of the criminal district court. In a previous case generated by the Comité des Citoyens, Ferguson had ruled that Louisiana's segregated rail-car Act was unconstitutional as applied to interstate trains, and that only the Federal government could regulate such matters. It was anticipated that a similar ruling would be made in the case involving Homer Plessy. However, Ferguson ruled that the state had a legal right to regulate intrastate railroads, of which the East Louisiana Railroad was an example. Thus the Louisiana legislature's passage of the Separate Car Act was both justifiable and legal. The Comité des Citoyens and Plessy appealed against Ferguson's decision to the Louisiana Supreme Court but lost there also. Finally, there was but one place left to turn: the US Supreme Court.

On 18 May 1896 the Supreme Court issued its controversial *Plessy v. Ferguson* decision. Judge Henry Billings Brown of Massachusetts stated: 'Legislation is powerless to eradicate racial instincts or to abolish distinctions based upon physical differences, and the attempt to do so can only result in accentuating the difficulties of the present situation.'[2] In a prophetic act of dissent, Associate Justice John M. Harlan denounced segregation, stating: 'Our Constitution is color blind.' None the less, the court upheld that separate accommodation did not deprive blacks of equal rights if that accommodation was equal. Unfortunately, separate facilities in most cases were not equal, and African Americans received fewer services, of lower quality. Applying to all public services and facilities throughout the South, this ruling was to stand as law in the United States until *Brown v. Board of Education of Topeka* in 1954.

Nearly all the other Southern states had passed Jim Crow laws by 1909. As a result, black travellers on railroad journeys throughout the South found themselves restricted to the Jim Crow car for hundreds of miles. Segregation was not limited to the 'partitioned coach', as many railroads tried to describe them politely. In dining cars heavy curtains were drawn across to create a mini-Jim Crow section. Although Pullman sleeping cars were specifically excluded from the Jim Crow laws, few black travellers could afford them. If they could, they were often assigned an open-section berth away from white passengers.

James Colvard, a retired railroad porter interviewed by Atlanta public radio station WRFG during the 1970s, recalled that black passengers travelling in Jim Crow coaches sometimes faced overcrowding. Once the Jim Crow section or car (usually at the front end of a passenger train) filled up, a decision had to be made. 'It was up to the white train conductor whether black passengers would stand or move back into the rest of the train if the first car got too crowded,' he observed.[3] Many times, black passengers found themselves standing.

In subsequent years Jim Crow laws would be extended to other forms of transportation, including buses, taxicabs, and airport waiting rooms. Though the laws were comparable to the Black Codes, segregation via Jim Crow was more harshly enforced. Laws were extended well beyond transportation – to schools and colleges, water fountains, sports and recreation facilities, public parks, orphanages, prisons, asylums, funeral homes, morgues, and cemeteries. According to historian C. Vann Woodward: 'The Jim Crow laws put the authority of the state or city in the voice of the street-car conductor, the railway brakeman, the bus driver, the theater usher, and also into the voice of the hoodlum of the public parks and playgrounds.'[4]

Education

The principle of 'separate but equal' was extended to education following the closure of Ware High School by the Richmond County Board of Education, in Georgia, in 1897. Named after Edmund Asa Ware, a Freedman's Bureau officer and president of Atlanta University, Ware High School was the first public high school for African Americans in Georgia, and one of only five in the South while it was in operation. In the face of protests that black students in the district were denied a high-school education in the public sector following its closure, the board of education argued that it could educate more African-American children at the primary level with the funds subsequently made available.

In response three black citizens of Augusta, Georgia – J. W. Cumming, James S. Harper, and John C. Ladeveze – brought a case against the board based upon the 14th Amendment guarantee of equal protection under the law. In the case of *Cumming v. Board of Education* of 1899, the plaintiffs claimed that the board was using the funds in its hands to assist in maintaining a high school for white children without providing a similar school for blacks. As a result, they demanded that the white high school in Richmond County be closed as well. However, the Supreme Court ruled that closing a white school would not help black students, and allowed the Ware High School closing to stand.

Following the decision in *Cumming v. Board of Education*, the flood gates were open for school boards throughout the South to reduce the education of black students to a bare minimum. Governor James Vardaman of Mississippi insisted that 'education is ruining our Negroes. They're demanding equality.' In 1912 a white school superintendent in the South observed:

> There has never been any serious attempt to offer adequate educational facilities for the colored race . . . [Some schools have] as many as 100 students to the teacher; no attempt is made to do more than teach the children to read, write, and figure, and these subjects are learned imperfectly.[5]

Voting rights

Although the 15th Amendment had prohibited the disenfranchisement of blacks, the Republican Party failed to put forth a clear position on 'enforcement' during the 1880s, and in 1890 Henry Cabot Lodge tried to introduce a measure to the House of Representatives providing for Federal supervision of elections. This attempt was blocked by Southern representatives, who dubbed it the 'Force Bill'. With the repeal of the enforcement laws in 1893, white Southerners felt free to disenfranchise black males on a state-by-state basis.

Mississippi had already begun this trend with the passage of new and elaborate suffrage qualifications in 1890. The constitution of Mississippi adopted that year contained two important sections on franchise. Section 241 provided that every qualified elector must have paid all taxes legally required of him for the two preceding years. A qualified elector must also have resided in the state for two years, and in the election district one year, prior to the election. Section 244 provided that every qualified elector must be able 'to read any section of the state Constitution or understand [the] same when read to him or give a reasonable interpretation thereof'. At a stroke the number of voting African Americans was restricted to a handful. By 1892 only eight thousand blacks remained on the voting rolls in Mississippi, and even these soon disappeared. The other Southern states followed suit.

Poll taxes and literacy tests also had the effect of depriving poor, illiterate whites of the vote. To circumvent this, seven Southern states enacted a constitutional device called a 'grandfather clause', which gave the vote to all male adults whose fathers or grandfathers had voted before 1 January 1867. As the former slaves were not officially granted the franchise until the adoption of the 15th Amendment in 1870, these clauses worked effectively to exclude blacks from the vote but assured the franchise to many impoverished and illiterate whites.

Black disenfranchisement received its ultimate legal sanction in the Supreme Court during a case called *Williams v. Mississippi* in 1898. In that year a black man named Williams was convicted of murder, but appealed on the grounds that he had been tried by an all-white jury and was therefore denied equal protection guaranteed under the 14th Amendment. As one had to be qualified to vote in order to serve on a jury in Mississippi, the Supreme Court upheld the literacy test, poll tax, and grandfather clause as voting qualifications because they did not openly indicate racial discrimination. State law was validated and the precedent was set for a host of similar measures.

By 1900 each Southern state had revised its constitution with an arsenal of Jim Crow electoral devices, including literacy tests, poll taxes, grandfather clauses, property requirements, and white primaries – all of which were designed to disenfranchise black voters. Not surprisingly, the number of Southern black voters plummeted. In Louisiana, for example, it fell from 130,000 in 1896 to 5,320 in 1900. The proportion of black voters in Georgia declined from 28.3 per cent of the total registered to vote in 1904 to 4.3 per cent in 1910. On the eve of the First World War the percentage of black males registered to vote in the Southern states ranged from approximately 2 to 15 per cent.

The 'Progressive' era

Beginning around 1900, the 'Progressive' era was an age of improvement for American society through education, political reform, business reform, and social welfare. However, although individual progressives such as Mary White Ovington and Ray Stannard Baker spoke out against racial injustice, the progressive movement as a whole did little as blacks continued to be lynched, disenfranchised, and discriminated against. Southern politicians, including Governor James K. Vardaman of Mississippi and Senator Ben Tillman of South Carolina, did support a variety of progressive policies. But their approach to reform, known as 'business progressivism', may be regarded as opportunistic because they believed that public health programmes and social reforms would attract business and industry into the South. However, they also incorporated disenfranchisement of blacks into their platforms as an essential element of social control.

Racism also pervaded the White House during the Progressive era. The age was heralded by a pistol shot that mortally wounded President William McKinley during September 1901. Ironically, the assassin was apprehended by a black, college-educated waiter called Parker. Within a week McKinley was dead and Theodore Roosevelt was sworn in as the new president. An energetic and youthful reformer who promised *all* Americans a 'square deal', Teddy Roosevelt dominated US politics for the next 12 years. Shortly after becoming president, he invited Booker T. Washington to a conference at the White House. Although previous presidents had also consulted the black educator, the Southern press took exception on this occasion. The New Orleans *Times Democrat* thundered: 'When Mr. Roosevelt sits down to dinner with a Negro he declares that the Negro is the social equal of the white man.' The normally fearless and impulsive president backed down on the race issue, and subsequently admitted that the dinner was 'a mistake'. Although Roosevelt and his successor, William Taft, continued to meet with Booker T. Washington, neither of them ate with him again. Indeed, Roosevelt commented that blacks were 'altogether inferior to the whites', while both leaders declined to speak out forcefully about the numerous lynching incidents that continued to be committed during their terms in office.

When the Democratic candidate Woodrow Wilson was voted into the White House in 1912, African Americans looked forward hopefully to what the new president termed his 'new freedom' for America. Although Wilson passed other Progressive reforms, which restricted monopolies and regulated interstate trade, he did nothing to alleviate the suffering of the blacks. A Southerner from Virginia, he exacerbated the situation by restoring segregation to the US Treasury and Post Office, which resulted in the erection of partitions between black and white officials and clerks, and the establishment of 'Jim Crow corners' with separate washrooms and lunchrooms for 'colored only'. When a group of black leaders led by Monroe Trotter, editor of the *Boston Guardian*, visited Wilson in 1913 to complain about his segregation of government employees, the president told them: 'Segregation is not humiliating but a benefit, and ought to be so regarded by you gentlemen.'[6]

Segregation in sport

Since the 1890s all professional sports had barred black participants. In the boxing world, white heavyweight champions drew the colour line and refused to fight black contenders. It took the controversial and uninhibited spirit of John Arthur Johnson of Galveston, Texas, better known as Jack Johnson, to challenge this. Johnson won 23 fights with only 1 loss, becoming the negro heavyweight champion in 1903. The white world heavyweight champion Jim Jeffries refused to step in the ring with the black champion, declaring 'I will not fight a negro!' Tommy Burns, who replaced Jeffries after he retired, agreed to a contest and was beaten by Johnson in the first heavyweight title bout between a white and a black man, held in Sydney, Australia, on 26 December 1908.

Jim Jeffries, the retired heavyweight champion, was subsequently asked to come out of retirement to reclaim the title. He was dubbed the 'Great White Hope', his task to 'save his race' by beating Johnson. In Reno, Nevada, on 4 July 1910 Jeffries was knocked out during the fifteenth round and Johnson became the undisputed world heavyweight champion. Jack Johnson's achievement in the world of boxing did much to raise African-American self-esteem, and paved the way for other black sportsmen and athletes to excel.

Although African Americans were not welcomed in the world of athletics during the post-Civil War years, the doors were opened to black athletes earlier than in other sports. In 1895 they were invited to qualify for the Penn relay in Philadelphia. However, they had to find their own sponsors and practice fields.

The early sponsors of most African-American athletes were segregated all-black secondary schools, black colleges and universities, and the 'colored' YMCAs. Prestigious Northern universities such as Harvard, Amherst, the University of Chicago, and Penn State also recruited African-American students among their track and field athletics teams. Listed as advocates and sponsors of African-American talent in track and field were all-black clubs like the Smart Set Club and the Vulcan Athletic League. Support from these organisations helped to make track and field an area where the black sportsperson could develop.

By 1890 the first African-American track star, William Tecumseh Sherman Jackson, emerged from the campus of Amherst College in Massachusetts as a half-miler. Between the years 1895 and 1897 Napoleon Bonaparte Marshall, of Harvard College, had run the 440-yard (400-metre) dash at 51.2 seconds. In 1907 John Baxter 'Doc' Taylor broke the Intercollegiate Amateur Athletic Association of America record for that distance with a time of 49.2 seconds. Taylor also won the first gold medal in the 4 by 400-metre (440-yard) relay during the 1908 Olympics held in England. During the years 1910 to 1918 Howard Porter Drew from Lexington, Virginia, became known as 'The World's Fastest Human'; he ran 100 metres (110 yards) in 10.8 seconds and the 70-yard (64-metre) sprint at 7.5 seconds on 8 June and 8 September 1912 respectively. Edward Solomon Butler set records in multiple track and field events that went unbroken at the University of Iowa until 1939. Later, the famed Jesse Owens set seven world records during his career that earned him four gold medals at the 1936 Berlin Olympics, while Adolf Hitler looked on.

In 1915 Princeton-born Paul Robeson won a four-year scholarship to Rutgers College (now University), New Jersey, in a state-wide written competition. Only the third African American to enter Rutgers, he went on to represent the college in football, baseball, basketball, and track events, as well as becoming an all-American professional footballer. Robeson later become a world-famous singer and actor. His starring role in *Othello* on Broadway in 1943 is considered a milestone in race relations. During the same year he received the Abraham Lincoln Medal for distinguished service in human relations. In 1951, as a representative of the Civil Rights Congress, he presented a petition to the United Nations charging the United States with genocide against blacks. Banned from public life in the United States because of his communist views, Robeson was eventually permitted to visit London and Moscow, where he continued to campaign for civil rights.

Invented by Abner Doubleday before the Civil War, baseball soared in popularity towards the end of the nineteenth century. Reflecting American society in general, amateur and professional baseball remained largely segregated. However, some inter-racial games occurred when major-league white teams played black teams in 'barnstorming' – or exhibition – games. Also, a small number of black players, including Moses Fleetwood 'Fleet' Walker, were included on white professional league team rosters during the period.

However, from about 1900 until 1947 segregation took its toll as 'colored' players, whether African American, Cuban, or Latin American, were barred from

Baseball star Jackie Robinson in Brooklyn Dodgers uniform.

the major leagues. As a result, blacks wishing to play the sport professionally had to create their own all-black leagues. Established in 1920 by Andrew 'Rube' Foster, the most viable of these was the Negro National League, which eventually included teams like the Kansas City Monarchs, the Birmingham Black Barons, and the New York Cubans. In Cuba, Mexico, and other parts of Latin America, baseball was not segregated. Many blacks played baseball there in the winter as well as in the negro leagues in the United States during the summer.

The negro leagues became filled with sportsmen of immense talent. Josh Gibson of the Pittsburgh Crawfords became known as the 'black Babe Ruth', hitting more than a thousand home runs. George 'Babe' Ruth Jr hit only 715. Pitcher Leroy 'Satchel' Paige claimed to have won two thousand games in his career.

The American Basketball Association was organised in 1925, but African Americans could not join. This was also the case with the Basketball Association of America, formed in 1946. The only venues open to black professional basketball players were the Harlem Globetrotters, the 'clown princes' of basketball, along with other segregated black teams.

All-black sports teams continued to be a constant reminder that segregation and inequality existed within American society. With fewer funds, they tended to offer lower salaries, and they played in smaller, less ornate ball parks and stadiums. These factors were a reminder that blacks were considered inferior by a dominant white society. On the other hand, they provided a source of pride, focus, and identity for the African-American community.

In the wake of the defeat of Nazi Germany and Fascist Italy and their abhorrent racial policies at the end of the Second World War, American professional sports finally became integrated. Black servicemen returning from Europe at the end of the war were not content with the continued racism and segregation at home. The first indication of changing attitudes came on 21 March 1946, when the Los Angeles Rams signed Kenny Washington and Woody Strode, two black football stars from University of California Los Angeles. The baseball colour barrier was finally breached on 10 April 1947 when Jackie Robinson was signed by Brooklyn Dodgers' co-owner Branch Rickey, and became the first African American to play in the major league.

Showing an early interest in civil rights, Robinson had worked for the desegregation of US armed forces after being drafted into the army in 1942. Assisted by the boxer Joe Louis, he campaigned for the opening to black soldiers of an officer candidate school. Following promotion to lieutenant, he faced a court martial for refusing to obey an order to move to the back of a military bus. Eventually he was exonerated because the order issued was considered a violation of army regulations. Nurtured by Branch Rickey, Robinson endured racial insults both on and off the field, and went on to win the *Sporting News* 'Rookie of the Year' award in 1947. Retiring from the sport in 1956, Jackie Robinson continued to battle against segregation, and was a member of the board of the National Association for the Advancement of Colored People until 1967.

Document case study

Jim Crow

4.1 The Supreme Court upholds segregation in *Plessy v. Ferguson*, 1896

We consider the underlying fallacy of the plaintiff's argument to consist in the assumption that the enforced separation of the two races stamps the colored race with a badge of inferiority . . . The argument also assumes that social prejudices may be overcome by legislation, and that equal rights cannot be secured to the Negro except by an enforced commingling of the two races . . .

Legislation is powerless to eradicate racial instincts or to abolish distinctions based upon physical differences, and the attempt to do so can only result in accentuating the difficulties of the present situation. If the civil and political rights of both races be equal one cannot be inferior to the other civilly or politically. If one race be inferior to the other socially, the Constitution of the United States cannot put them upon the same plane.

Source: US Information Service, based on *US statutes at large*, Washington DC: US Government Printing Office, 1896, vol. 163, chapter 537; Gilder Lehrman Institute of American History collection

4.2 Judge John Harlan, the only member of the Supreme Court who believed that segregation in railway cars was unconstitutional, expresses his views in 1896

The white race deems itself to be the dominant race in this country . . . But in view of the Constitution . . . there is in this country no superior, dominant, ruling class of citizens. There is no caste here. Our Constitution is color-blind, and neither knows nor tolerates classes among citizens. In respects of civil rights, all citizens are equal before the law.

Source: US Information Service, based on *US statutes at large*, Washington DC: US Government Printing Office, 1896, vol. 163, chapter 537; Gilder Lehrman Institute of American History collection

4.3 In response to the introduction of a 'Jim Crow' street-car law in New Orleans in 1902, blacks tried to organise their own transportation

. . . An association of women attached to the Masonic Order proposed to run bus lines to accommodate Negro passengers, and issued a call to the fifty Negro organizations in New Orleans to send representatives to a meeting at which the question would be considered. Unfeasible as the scheme was, it nevertheless appealed strongly to the Negroes, and at the meetings representatives from nearly all the organizations were present.

It was apparent from the discussions that the 'ruling passion' back of it all was a sense of deep humiliation that Negroes as a race should be considered unworthy to ride in conveyances with white people. The railway companies had announced their intention of putting wire screens in every car, and to have Negroes occupy the rear seats. This idea of sitting behind screens, as if they were wild or obnoxious animals, was another fact contributing to their mortification. Many of them, it was said, took pride in keeping clean, in wearing good clothes, and in behaving well, as much because they could feel at ease in decent company as because it gave them other personal satisfaction. To exclude such Negroes from compartments occupied by white people would, they said, be as unjust as it would be to force them to sit in compartments with unworthy representatives of their own race, whom they, as much as the white people, despised. It would be equally unjust to admit obnoxious white people to white compartments and exclude respectable Negroes from enjoying the same privilege.

Probably the next most pronounced sentiment of the meetings was a demand for Negroes to support one another in business enterprises. To the Negroes, the strongest argument in favor of a bus line was the fact that it would be a Negro enterprise supported by Negro capital and conducted for the general benefit of the race in New Orleans. Out of this session grew many an urgent appeal for Negroes to acquire property and contribute to the general welfare of other Negroes by patronizing them in their businesses. This sentiment is growing stronger and stronger every day, and the results of it are more and more apparent. Negroes no longer wish to send their children to white teachers; Negro patients demand the services of Negro physicians; drugstores, saloons, grocery-stores, coal and wood shops—in fact, almost every retail business in the city—are conducted on a small scale by Negroes, and patronized almost exclusively by members of that race.

Source: A. R. Holcombe, 'The separate street-car law in New Orleans', *Outlook*, 29 November 1902, pp. 746–47

4.4 Speech delivered in 1914 by the governor of Mississippi, James K. Vardaman, who did much to stir up racial hatred

I do not think it was ever intended by the Creator that the two races should live together upon equal terms . . . One or the other must rule. The people of the South tried to share with the Negro the government of the country after the war, but the Negro declined to share with the white man. Black heels rested cruelly upon white necks for many years after the close of the war. The white man endured the Negro's misrule, his insolence, impudence, and infamy. He suffered his criminal incapacity to govern until the public domain had been well-nigh squandered and the public treasury looted . . . We invoked the law of self-preservation; we arose in the might of an outraged race and . . . the southern white man drove from power the scalawag, the carpetbagger, and the incompetent Negro.

Source: Gilder Lehrman Institute of American History collection

4.5 Transcript of a meeting between President Wilson and a black delegation who were protesting about the segregation of Federal employees in 1914

[William Monroe Trotter, executive secretary of the National Equal Rights League] Mr. President, we are here to renew our protest against the segregation of colored employees in the departments of our National Government. We [had] appealed to you to undo this race segregation in accord with your duty as President and with your pre-election pledges to colored American voters. We stated that such segregation was a public humiliation and degradation, and entirely unmerited and far-reaching in its injurious effect . . .

[President Woodrow Wilson] The white people of the country, as well as I, wish to see the colored people progress, and admire the progress they have already made, and want to see them continue along independent lines. There is, however, a great prejudice against colored people . . . It will take one hundred years to eradicate this prejudice, and we must deal with it as practical men. Segregation is not humiliating but a benefit, and ought to be so regarded by you gentlemen. If your organization goes out and tells the colored people of the country that it is a humiliation, they will so regard it, but if you do not tell them so, and regard it rather as a benefit, they will regard it the same. The only harm that will come will be if you cause them to think it is a humiliation.

Source: *The Crisis*, vol. 9 (January 1915), p. 120

4.6 Extract from a speech by Branch Rickey, owner of the Brooklyn Dodgers, to the One Hundred Percent Wrong Club banquet in Atlanta, Georgia, on 20 January 1956

I had to get the right man . . . I couldn't come with a man to break down a tradition that had in it centered and concentrated all the prejudices of a great many people north and south unless he was good. He must justify himself upon the positive principle of merit. He must be a great player. I must not risk an excuse of trying to do something in the sociological field, or in the race field, just because of sort of a 'holier than thou'. I must be sure that the man was good on the field, but more dangerous to me, at that time, and even now, is the wrong man off the field. It didn't matter to me so much in choosing a man off the field that he was temperamental,—righteously subject to resentments. I wanted a man of exceptional intelligence, a man who was able to grasp and control the responsibilities of himself to his race and could carry that load.

Source: Library of Congress, Manuscript Division, Branch Rickey Papers

Document case-study questions

1 Compare the response of the Supreme Court to racial issues in Documents 4.1 and 4.2.

2 What can be learned from Document 4.3 about the black response to 'Jim Crow'?

3 Explain what you understand by the phrase 'We invoked the law of self-preservation' in Document 4.4.

4 What can we learn from Document 4.5 about the opposition there was to desegregation?

5 What did Branch Rickey mean in Document 4.6 by getting 'the right man'?

Notes and references

1 Keith Weldon Medley, 'The sad story of how "separate but equal" was born', *Smithsonian* (February 1994), pp. 106, 112.

2 *Plessy v. Ferguson*, 163 US 537 (1896).

3 Clifford M. Kuhn, Harlon E. Joye, and E. Bernard West, *Living Atlanta: an oral history of the city, 1914–1948*, Atlanta, Georgia, 1990, p. 62.

4 C. Vann Woodward, *The strange career of Jim Crow*, New York, 1955, p. 107.

5 William Loren Katz, *Eyewitness: the negro in American history*, New York: Pittman Publishing Corporation, 1967, p. 376.

6 *The Crisis*, vol. 9 (January 1915), p. 120.

5 Early black protest

Early black leaders

The African-American community responded to the Jim Crow laws in divergent ways. The majority of Southern blacks, particularly those who supported the pacifism of Booker T. Washington, realised that they could get social, economic, and political redress for their grievances by relying solely on white goodwill. Many more sustained the notion of dignity and racial pride through family role models. Others, such as the advocates of W. E. B. Du Bois and Marcus Garvey, adopted a more militant stance and practised individual acts of 'day-to-day' resistance, or turned to radical organisations and faced violent repression.

Booker T. Washington

Booker Taliaferro Washington was born a slave in Virginia around 1856. At the age of 16 he enrolled at the Hampton Agricultural Institute, a freedman's school founded at Hampton, Virginia, by Samuel Chapman Armstrong. A commander of black troops during the Civil War, Armstrong later served as a Freedmen's Bureau agent, before founding the Hampton Institute in 1868. It combined instruction in manual labour with teacher training, reflecting Armstrong's belief in educating 'the hand, the head, and the heart'. He created an educational system which he thought would enable African Americans, and other disenfranchised peoples, to rise gradually to the social level of whites. Becoming Washington's mentor, Armstrong eventually employed the young black on his staff to educate Native Americans as part of a programme to 'civilise' the recently defeated Plains Indians.[1]

In 1881 Lewis Adams, a black political leader in Macon County, Georgia, agreed to help two white Democratic Party candidates, William Foster and Arthur Brooks, to win a local election in return for the building of a school for blacks in the area. Both men were elected and they then used their influence to secure approval for the building of what became the Tuskegee Normal and Industrial Institute in Alabama. Samuel Armstrong was asked to recommend a white teacher to take charge of the new school. Instead he suggested Booker T. Washington, who received the appointment.

Following in the footsteps of his mentor, Washington modelled the Tuskegee Institute, opened in 1888, on the Hampton school. Believing that blacks could benefit more from vocational training than from a college education, he taught

Booker T. Washington, first principal of the Tuskegee Institute, who accepted segregation and appealed for blacks to work in harmony with whites.

specific trades such as carpentry, farming, and mechanical engineering. Most blacks still lived in poverty in the rural South, and Washington felt they should learn skills, work hard, and save money to buy property. He predicted that blacks would be granted civil and political rights after gaining a strong economic foundation, and explained these theories in his book *Up from slavery*, published in 1901.

The beginnings at Tuskegee were humble and the first efforts were in agriculture with what Booker T. Washington described as 'one hoe and a blind mule'.[2] A loan of $500 from the Hampton Institute enabled him to buy a farm of 40 hectares (100 acres). He worked hard to raise the money to pay back the loan, meet the payments on land and buildings, and extend the farm. By 1900 the school owned nearly 1,000 hectares (2,460 acres). By the third year student enrolment rose from 30 to 169, and by 1894 it had reached 712, with 54 officers and teachers.[3] The institute earned $11,679 during the first two years. This almost doubled in the third year, and after 14 years it was receiving about $80,000 annually. Within 30 years the campus grew from 3 rough wooden cabins to 60 buildings, including classrooms and dormitories. All but four of these had been built by students as part of their industrial education.

As the Tuskegee Institute expanded, Washington spent much of his time fundraising, and the institute became famous as a model of industrial education. In order to reduce racial conflict, he advised blacks to stop demanding equal rights and learn to live a separate existence from white people. He also urged whites to give blacks better jobs and opportunities. In the spring of 1895 Washington suddenly rose to national prominence when he gave a well-received speech on industrial education at Fisk University in Nashville, Tennessee. A reporter for the Nashville *American* proclaimed it a 'complete success', and compared Washington to Frederick Douglass as a 'benefactor to the Negro race'.[4]

At the Atlanta Cotton States and International Exposition in September 1895, blacks were invited to display their products and, as the Tuskegee and Hampton institutes had the largest number of black exhibits, Washington was invited to deliver an address at the opening ceremony. This was the first occasion on which a black man spoke publicly on the same platform as whites in the Southern states. In this speech Washington chose his words very carefully, owing to the predominantly white Southern audience. He spoke against agitation for social equality and recommended acceptance of segregation, declaring: 'In all things that are purely social we can be as separate as the fingers, yet one as the hand in all things essential to mutual progress.'

Although Washington was labelled an 'accommodationist' and much criticised by Northern blacks, the 'Atlanta Compromise' speech had tremendous power, and in the context of the times it probably did much to improve friendship and the working relationship between the races. Washington went on to become a shrewd political leader, advising not only presidents but also members of Congress and governors on political appointments for blacks and sympathetic whites. He also urged wealthy people to contribute to various black organisations and, with T. Thomas Fortune, in 1900 founded the National Negro Business League to help black businesses.

Throughout his life Washington tried to please whites in both the North and the South through his public actions and his speeches. However – according to his most recent biographer, Louis Harlan – he had a 'secret life' in which he engaged in a series of covert civil rights activities, sponsoring anti-segregation law-suits and publishing anonymous critical editorials in the black press. None the less, the influence of Samuel Armstrong is clear throughout his work. Indeed, recent studies such as Robert Francis Engs's *Educating the disfranchised and disinherited* (1999) have blamed Armstrong for Washington's failings as a civil rights leader, and for 'mis-educating' an entire generation of African Americans.

W. E. B. Du Bois

Contemporary opposition to Booker T. Washington came chiefly from the likes of Northern blacks such as William Monroe Trotter and George Washington Forbes, editors of the *Boston Guardian*, who regularly criticised him for being too conservative and deferential to white opinion. Washington's most persuasive critic was the black intellectual and historian W. E. B. Du Bois, who attacked his educational and political philosophy and practices. Born on 23 February 1868, William Edward Burghardt Du Bois was raised in a small black community in Massachusetts called Great Barrington. He graduated from high school early and enrolled at Fisk University. Upon receiving his bachelor's degree, he accepted a scholarship at the University of Berlin, where he studied for two years. Following this he went to Harvard, where in 1895 he received his doctoral degree, being the first African American to do so. Published as *The suppression of the African slave trade to the United States of America, 1638–1870*, his dissertation is regarded as a masterpiece of historiography, and remains an outstanding example of his scholarship. From 1896 to 1910 Du Bois was professor of economics and history at Atlanta University, a black institution that competed with Tuskegee for contributions from Northern philanthropists.

In 1903 Du Bois challenged the basic ideas of Booker T. Washington in an essay entitled 'Of Mr Booker T. Washington and others', published in his book *The souls of black folk* (1903). Offering a programme of action very similar to that employed later during the civil rights movement of the 1960s, Du Bois attacked Washington's 'accommodationist' political views and demanded that blacks must openly strive for their rights. He argued that African Americans needed to fight to win equal justice, and that an educated black elite (the 'talented tenth') should lead blacks in the United States and in Africa to freedom. He criticised what he regarded as Washington's surrender of civil rights and human dignity for economic gain. Du Bois also challenged the ways in which Washington used his power. By controlling many black newspapers, for example, Washington made it difficult for differing views on the struggle for civil rights to be published. Furthermore, because Washington was acclaimed as the foremost black leader, he helped determine which racial policies and practices were acceptable.

Organised black resistance

National Association for the Advancement of Colored People

The first active black resistance to segregation and racism was organised by the National Afro-American League, founded by T. Thomas Fortune in 1887. The league worked against the political and civil suppression of the black person's rights in the South. It also fought inequalities in education and the prison system, and attacked discrimination in public places throughout the nation. Although Fortune's tone was militant, he urged the use of peaceful methods. Afro-American leadership responded positively in the press and in organised meetings. On the other hand, the white Southern press denounced the idea as a vehicle for perpetuating racial tension. Despite its original enthusiasm, the league failed to make the impact that Fortune hoped for on a national level – although there were successes at local level. A lack of support from national leaders such as Frederick Douglass and John Langston also contributed to its decline, but inadequate financial support was the major cause of the league's failure.

Fortune went on to found the Afro-American Council on 15 September 1898, but when Booker T. Washington began to influence this organisation the latter's opponents looked elsewhere for inspiration. In 1905 they met under the leadership of W. E. B. Du Bois on the Canadian side of Niagara Falls – the hotels on the US side would not accept them. Soon known as the Niagara Movement, they met again the next year at Harper's Ferry.

Tragic events rapidly gave the Niagara Movement valuable white support. In August 1908 violent race riots broke out in Springfield, Illinois, within a few blocks of Abraham Lincoln's birthplace. Two blacks were lynched, six more were murdered by other means, and over two thousand African Americans were forced to leave the city. William English Walling, a German-Jewish reporter, investigated the story for his paper, the *Independent*, informing his readers that the 'spirit of Lincoln . . . must be revived'.

Meanwhile, a small group of white reformers had also become disenchanted with Washington's cautious approach. Prominent among them was newspaper publisher Oswald Garrison Villard, grandson of abolitionist William Lloyd Garrison. On the hundredth anniversary of Lincoln's birthday this group united with the Niagara Movement to call for civil rights and resistance against racist attacks. Shortly afterwards, on 12 February 1909, they formed the multiracial National Association for the Advancement of Colored People (NAACP). Membership consisted of leading black intellectuals such as journalist Ida Wells-Barnett, educator Mary Church Terrell, and churchman Archibald H. Grimké; as well as prominent white intellectuals like writer Lincoln Steffens and reformer Jane Addums. As a founding father of the NAACP, W. E. B. Du Bois edited the organisation's journal, *The Crisis*, from its inception in 1910 to his initial resignation from the organisation in 1934. On his return to the NAACP in 1944, Du Bois also served as director of special research.

Integration of the races was the goal and practice of the NAACP from the moment of its inception. The principal technique adopted by this organisation was the use of the Constitution and the court system of the United States to achieve civil rights for African Americans by legal means. The NAACP began to develop grassroots black support, with 274 branches and over 90,000 members by the early 1920s. Despite this progress, it continued to be perceived by many as an elitist and largely white-run organisation, and did not achieve a truly mass membership until the 1940s.

Ida B. Wells-Barnett

The NAACP – plus other organisations such as the National Association of Colored Women (NACW), the Council for Interracial Co-operation (CIC), and the Association of Southern Women for the Prevention of Lynching (ASWPL) – launched an anti-lynching campaign that would span 30 years. These groups lobbied Congress to state publicly that lynching was a clear violation of constitutional guarantees. The NAACP placed full-page advertisements in the *New York Times*, the *Atlanta Constitution*, and other newspapers during 1922, denouncing the practice of lynching and calling it the 'shame of America'. The statistics were appalling. At least 3,224 people had been murdered by lynching by 1918. Undoubtedly, the real number was much higher for many lynching incidents were not reported by local authorities.

A leading crusader against lynching was Ida B. Wells-Barnett, a journalist and newspaper editor in Memphis, Tennessee. After three successful grocery-store owners were lynched in 1892, Wells-Barnett began to campaign against lynching and to write about the culture of the South. Her accounts of racism in the South gained her a national audience. Like W. E. B. Du Bois, she disagreed with Booker T. Washington and was among the first women to join the NAACP. Later in life she broke with the NAACP, considering it too timid, and supported the controversial Marcus Garvey and his calls for black pride, if not his back-to-Africa movement.

Ida Wells-Barnett was a prominent black journalist. She conducted an investigation into the practice of lynching and published the results in local newspapers, using the pen name Iola. She discovered that out of 728 black men who were lynched by white mobs almost 70 per cent were killed for minor offences. In 1889 she became co-editor, with the Reverend R. Nightingale, of a newspaper called the *Free Speech and Headlight* which championed the cause of justice for blacks. Her life was threatened, and her office was demolished many times. Eventually she was forced out of the South, but she continued her work against Southern mob rule.

In 1898 Wells-Barnett wrote a letter to President McKinley appealing for Federal intervention in the South to stop the illegal practice of lynching. She declared: 'Nowhere in the civilized world save the United States of America do men, possessing all civil and political power, go out in bands of 50 to 5,000 to hunt down, shoot, hang or burn to death an individual, unarmed and absolutely powerless.' In 1901 she published a book entitled *Lynching and the excuse*, which became widely circulated and well known for its articulate and passionate denunciation of lynching.

Hopeful signs of a breakthrough in the legal battle against lynching were dashed in 1906. In that year a sheriff and two of his deputies in Chattanooga, Tennessee, were sentenced to only 60 days in jail for permitting a black man named Ed Johnson to be lynched, after the Supreme Court allowed an appeal in the case and directed all proceedings to be stayed. Public outrage continued, and lynching steadily decreased, with little help from the Federal government. The Supreme Court considered the lynching crisis to be a local problem, and preferred to let the individual states handle it. By the end of 1932 the number of lynchings had declined to a new low of 10 incidents per annum; during the entire decade of the 1930s only 88 cases were reported. In the early 1930s Congress proposed the Costigan-Wagner Bill that proposed Federal trials for any law enforcement officers who failed to exercise their responsibilities during a lynching incident. The bill was not passed, despite overwhelming public support. A national poll taken in 1937 found that 65 per cent of all Southerners supported legislation that would have made lynching a Federal crime.[5]

Marcus Garvey

With the death of Booker T. Washington in November 1915, a vacuum was created in African-American leadership which W. E. B. Du Bois, and the other black intellectuals of the day, failed to fill. Within a year of Washington's death a West Indian named Marcus Mosiah Garvey Jr had taken his place. Born on 17 August 1887 in St Ann's Bay, Jamaica, Garvey left school at 14 and worked as a printer before becoming involved in the Jamaican nationalist movement. After touring Central America and spending time in London, he returned to Jamaica in 1914 and established the Universal Negro Improvement Association (UNIA). This organisation adopted the philosophy of integration, initially intending to promote industrial education as practised by Washington at the Tuskegee Institute. Short of money, Garvey embarked on a fund-raising tour of the United States in 1916. A powerful and charismatic public speaker, he quickly gained a following for 'Garveyism' among the African-American community during a period when race riots and general anti-black feeling were rife. In 1917 he established a branch of UNIA in Harlem, New York, and within a year had recruited about a thousand members. He also began publication of a weekly newspaper, *The Negro World*, which soon gained a wide circulation in the United States, South America, the Caribbean, and Africa.

During 1919 Garvey began several money-making initiatives which he hoped would enrich and strengthen UNIA. The Negro Factories Corporation promoted black-run business and ran a chain of retail outlets. The more ambitious Black Star Line, an international black steamship company, raised funds by selling certificates for shares valued at $750,000 to thousands of black small investors. Buying three ships, Garvey visualised a business venture which would unite black peoples worldwide in international commerce. The line's flagship, the SS *Yarmouth*, made its maiden voyage in November 1919 and two other ships joined the line in 1920.

As his popularity and power increased, Garvey grew away from the philosophy of Booker T. Washington, becoming a black nationalist who believed that African Americans should develop their own institutions and minimise contact with whites. His ultimate ambition was to end colonialism and to establish an independent black African empire. Delegates from 24 countries gathered at the UNIA First International Convention of the Negro Peoples of the World, held in Harlem during August 1920. Elected provisional president of the anticipated new black state, Garvey created a black nobility called the Knights of the Nile, and developed several associations, including a black paramilitary group called the Universal African Legion and a nursing organisation known as the Black Cross.

From 1920 to 1924 W. E. B. Du Bois published in *The Crisis* a series of articles that were very critical of Garvey. He attacked Garvey's 'Back to Africa' project as being insensitive and unrealistic. He was particularly concerned that this venture might become confused with his own more thoughtful pan-African philosophy, which promoted the idea of the unification of all Africans into a single African state. Of mixed racial origin, Du Bois was also concerned that Garvey was attempting to instil inappropriate 'black supremacist' West Indian values and attitudes into African-American society.

Some black American spokespersons, such as labour leader Asa Philip Randolph and NAACP leader William Pickens, were initially prepared to support Garvey. But this support dwindled rapidly when in June 1922 he met with Ku Klux Klan leader Edward Young Clarke in an attempt to expand UNIA's influence in the South, where most blacks still lived. As Garveyism and the hooded white order shared beliefs in racial pride and separatism, Garvey attempted to justify this liaison as 'a realistic appraisal of race American relations'.[6] Black leaders were further infuriated when they learned that Garvey, at a speaking engagement in New Orleans, remarked that, because black people had not built the railroad system, they should not insist on riding in the same cars as white patrons.

During the early 1920s the Garvey movement began to buckle under the strains of internal dissension, opposition from black critics, and government harassment. By 1922 the Black Star Line was bankrupt, and in 1925 the Federal government indicted Garvey for mail fraud after he continued to advertise shares in the company. The UNIA leader's fate was sealed when NAACP leaders launched a 'Garvey must go' campaign. Found guilty as charged, Garvey began a five-year prison sentence at the Atlanta Federal penitentiary. His sentence was commuted after three years and he was deported back to Jamaica in November 1927, following which he never returned to the United States. Back in his home country, Garvey reconstituted UNIA. He held conventions there and in Canada, while the remains of his original movement stumbled on in the United States without him. Dabbling in local politics, Garvey remained a keen observer of world events and he wrote voluminously. He moved to London in 1935, shortly before Fascist Italy invaded Abyssinia. Haile Selassie snubbed Garvey on his arrival in England, and Garvey's subsequent public criticism of the exiled Abyssinian emperor alienated many of his remaining followers. During his last years Garvey slid into such obscurity that he suffered the final indignity of reading his own obituaries in the London newspapers a month before his death during the German bombing of London on 10 June 1940.

Document case study

Early black protest

5.1 Speech given by Booker T. Washington at the Atlanta Exposition in 1895, subsequently known as the Atlanta Compromise

A ship lost at sea for many days suddenly sighted a friendly vessel. From the mast of the unfortunate vessel was seen a signal, 'Water, water; we die of thirst!' The answer from the friendly vessel at once came back, 'Cast down your bucket where you are.'

The captain of the distressed vessel, at last heeding the injunction, cast down his bucket, and it came up full of fresh, sparkling water . . . To those of my race who underestimate the importance of cultivating friendly relations with the southern white man, who is their next-door neighbor, I would say: 'Cast down your bucket where you are'—cast it down in making friends in every manly way of the people of all races by whom we are surrounded.

Cast it down in agriculture, mechanics, in commerce, in domestic service, and in the professions . . . Our greatest danger is that in the great leap from slavery to freedom we may overlook the fact that the masses of us are to live by the productions of our hands, and fail to keep in mind that we shall prosper in proportion as we learn to dignify and glorify common labour and put brains and skill into the common occupations of life; shall prosper in proportion as we learn to draw the line between the superficial and the substantial, the ornamental gewgaws of life and the useful. No race can prosper till it learns that there is as much dignity in tilling a field as in writing a poem. It is at the bottom of life we must begin, and not at the top . . .

The wisest among my race understand that the agitation of questions of social equality is the extremist folly, and that progress in the enjoyment of all the privileges that will come to us must be the result of severe and constant struggle rather than of artificial forcing. No race that has anything to contribute to the markets of the world is long in any degree ostracized. It is important and right that all privileges of the law be ours, but it is vastly more important that we be prepared for the exercise of these privileges. The opportunity to earn a dollar in a factory just now is worth infinitely more than the opportunity to spend a dollar in an opera-house.

Source: Booker T. Washington, *Up from slavery: an autobiography*, New York, 1901, pp. 218–21

5.2 The black scholar W. E. B. Du Bois responds to Booker T. Washington

Easily the most striking thing in the history of the American Negro since 1876 is the ascendancy of Mr. Booker T. Washington . . . His programme of industrial education, conciliation of the South, and submission and silence as to civil and political rights was not wholly original . . . But Mr. Washington first indissolubly linked these things; he . . . changed it from a by-path into a veritable Way of Life . . .

Mr. Washington represents in Negro thought the old attitude of adjustment and submission; but adjustment at such a peculiar time as to make his programme unique. This is an age of unusual economic development, and Mr. Washington's programme naturally takes an economic cast, becoming a gospel of Work and Money to such an extent as apparently almost completely to overshadow the higher aims of life . . . Mr. Washington's programme practically accepts the alleged inferiority of the Negro races . . . In the history of nearly all other races and peoples the doctrine preached at such crises has been that manly self-respect is worth more than lands and houses, and that a people who voluntarily surrender such respect, or cease striving for it, are not worth civilizing.

. . . Mr. Washington distinctly asks that black people give up, at least for the present, three things, –

First, political power.

Second, insistence on civil rights.

Third, higher education of Negro youth.

. . . The question then comes: Is it possible, and probable, that nine millions of men can make effective progress in economic lines if they are deprived of political rights, made a servile caste, and allowed only the most meagre chance for developing their exceptional men? If history and reason give any distinct answer to these questions, it is an emphatic No . . .

Source: W. E. B. Du Bois, 'Of Mr Booker T. Washington and others' (1903), reprinted in W. E. B. Du Bois, *The souls of black folk: essays and sketches*, New York: New American Library, 1969, pp. 41–52

5.3 Ida Wells-Barnett describes her views on lynching

A word as to the charge itself. In considering the third reason assigned by the Southern white people for the butchery of blacks, the question must be asked, what the white man means when he charges the black man with rape. Does he mean the crime which the statutes of the states describe as such? Not by any means. With the Southern white man, any misalliance existing between a white woman and a colored man is a sufficient foundation for the charge of rape. The Southern white man says that it is impossible for a voluntary alliance to exist between a white woman and a colored man, and therefore, the fact of an alliance is a proof of force. In numerous instances where colored men have been lynched on the charge of rape, it was positively known at the time of lynching, and indisputably proven after the victim's death, that the relationship sustained between the man and the woman was voluntary and clandestine, and that in no court of law could even the charge of assault have been successfully maintained.

Source: Ida Wells-Barnett, *A red record*, Chicago: Donohue & Hermeberry, 1895, p. 8

5.4 An editorial by Ida Wells-Barnett

We plead not for the colored people alone, but for all victims of the terrible injustice which puts men and women to death without form of law. During the year 1894, there were 132 persons executed in the United States by due form of law, while in the same year, 197 persons were put to death by mobs, who gave the victims no opportunity to make a lawful defense. No comment need be made upon a condition of public sentiment responsible for such alarming results.

Source: *Free Speech*, 21 May 1892

5.5 Marcus Garvey, believing he was a black Moses chosen to lead his people back to Africa, explains his beliefs to white Americans

The Negro must have a country, and a nation of his own. If you laugh at the idea, then you are selfish and wicked, for you and your children do not intend that the Negro shall discommode you in yours. If you do not intend to give him equal opportunities in yours; then it is plain to see that you mean that he must die, even as the Indian to make room for your generations.

Why should the Negro die? Has he not borne the burden of civilization in this Western world for three hundred years? Has he not contributed his best to America? Surely all this stands to his credit, but there will not be enough room and the one answer is 'find a place'. We have found a place, it is Africa and as black men for three centuries have helped white men build America, surely generous and grateful white men will help black men build Africa . . .

Source: From a magazine article quoted by Marcus Garvey, *An appeal to the soul of white America*, Baltimore: Soper Library, Morgan State University, 1923, n.p.

5.6 Editorial by Marcus Garvey

ITALY'S CONQUEST?

Mussolini of Italy has conquered Haile Selassie of Abyssinia, but he has not conquered the Abyssinians; nor Abyssinia. The Emperor of Abyssinia allowed himself to be conquered, by playing white, by trusting to white advisers and by relying on white Governments, including the white League of Nations.

We can remember in 1920 inviting the Government of Abyssinia to send representatives to the International Convention of the Negro Peoples of the world in common with other Negro Governments, institutions and organizations. Whilst others replied, and most of them sent representatives to that greatest of all Negro Conventions, the Abyssinian Government returned the communication unopened. Its policy then, as during the Italo-Abyssinian war, was no doubt to rely completely on the advice and friendship of white people. They ignored Negro relationship[s] from without and throttled Negro aspirations from within. The result was that they dragged along without any racial policy, except that of the ruling classes, believing themselves white and better than the rest, with a right to suppress the darker elements which make up the tremendous population.

Source: *The Black Man*, London, July/August 1936

Document case-study questions

1 Explain the conflicting strategies to achieve full racial equality outlined in Documents 5.1 and 5.2.

2 Comment on Ida Wells-Barnett's reaction to lynching in Document 5.3.

3 Evaluate Ida Well-Barnett's contribution to the struggle for racial equality, based on your knowledge and on her editorial comments in Document 5.4.

4 What point is Marcus Garvey making in Document 5.5?

5 Explain Garvey's position on the Italian conquest of Abyssinia as outlined in Document 5.6.

Notes and references

1 Booker T. Washington, *Up from slavery: an autobiography*, New York, 1901, p. 51.

2 Booker T. Washington, 'Industrial education for the negro', *The negro problem*, New York: James Pott & Company, 1903, p. 20.

3 *The story of my life and work: Booker T. Washington papers*, Toronto, 1901, vol. 1, 'The autobiographical writings', pp. 13–15.

4 *Booker T. Washington papers*, vol. 1, pp. 61–64.

5 Stewart E. Tolnay and E. M. Beck, *A festival of violence: an analysis of Southern lynchings, 1882–1930*, Urbana and Chicago: University of Illinois Press, p. 202.

6 Kevern Verney, *Black civil rights in America*, New York: Routledge, 2000, p. 21.

6 Impact of war

The First World War

On 2 April 1917, after three years attempting to maintain a neutral foreign policy, President Woodrow Wilson asked Congress to declare war on Germany. 'The world,' he declared, 'must be made safe for democracy.' Participation in the war effort was problematic for African Americans. While America was embarking on a crusade to make the world safe for democracy abroad, it continued to neglect the fight for equality at home. Three months after the United States declared war, 15,000 blacks conducted a silent parade in New York City, carrying signs to protest against the continued lynchings and the race riots in American cities. One sign read 'Mr. President, why not make America safe for democracy?'

Leaders of the black community differed in their responses to the war crisis. Labour pioneer Asa Philip Randolph was pessimistic about what it would mean for black Americans, pointing out that they had sacrificed their blood on the battlefields of every American war since the revolution, but it had still not brought them full citizenship. Uncharacteristically, W. E. B. Du Bois argued that 'while the war lasts [we should] forget our special grievances and close our ranks shoulder to shoulder with our white fellow citizens and the allied nations that are fighting for democracy'.[1] America's black population decided to close ranks, and blacks were among the first to volunteer and serve.

However, as only 75,000 volunteers of all ethnic backgrounds answered the call to arms, conscription had to be introduced via the Selective Service Act on 18 May 1917. The US Army drafted both black and white men, but they served in segregated units. A total of 380,000 African Americans joined the US Army during the war. Approximately 200,000, of whom 42,000 saw combat, were sent to Europe. The remainder were assigned to labour and stevedore battalions, performing essential duties in support of front-line troops, such as digging trenches and building roads and bridges.

Regarding the other branches of service, blacks were barred from the Marine Corps and the Coast Guard. Enlisted rates, or ranks, in the US Navy had remained generally open to men of all races after the Civil War, but African Americans had been actively pushed into becoming officers' stewards since the 1880s.

Initially, African Americans were refused training as army officers but, after the NAACP organised protests, the army finally agreed to begin Reserve Officer

Training Corps programmes at several black colleges, and established a segregated officers' training school at Fort Des Moines, Iowa, in 1917. By the end of the war in November 1918, more than 639 African-American officers had led their fellow black troops through some of the bitterest campaigns of the conflict.

'Over there'

American troops arrived in Europe at a crucial moment in the war. Russia had just signed an armistice with Germany, in December 1917, which permitted the Germans to concentrate their forces on the Western Front. If Germany could stage a huge offensive before the Americans came to the aid of the war-weary allies, it might yet win the war.

Two divisions of African-American soldiers were included within the American Expeditionary Force sent to France. Despite his earlier praise of black troops while serving as a junior officer in the 10th US Cavalry during the 1890s, General John J. Pershing introduced segregation to the trenches by loaning his black combat troops of the 93rd Division to the French army. Desperate for reinforcements, and used to fighting alongside their own African colonial forces, the 16th French Division welcomed their black American comrades.

Nicknamed the Harlem Hellfighters, the 369th Infantry Regiment (formerly the 15th Regiment New York National Guard) fought alongside the French at Château-Thierry and Belleau Wood during June 1918. They subsequently proved their worth by driving the Germans back at the Argonne Forest and the Meuse

A wounded African-American veteran of the 369th Infantry, with his family, watches the 1919 victory parade in New York City.

River. In total, they spent 191 days in the front line – longer than any other American unit in the war. The regiment became one of the most highly decorated black units when it returned home at the end of the war.

During May 1918 Privates Henry Johnson and Needham Roberts alone stood off the attack of a much larger German force, and in the process killed four and wounded several other enemy soldiers. As a result, Johnson and Roberts became the first American 'doughboys', white or black, to be awarded the French Croix de Guerre. In August 1918 Sergeant William Butler won the US Army's Distinguished Service Cross for single-handedly putting another German raiding party to flight. One hundred and seventy-one other officers and men of the regiment also earned individual medals, while the whole unit received the Croix de Guerre for taking Sechault on 29 September 1918. Three other black regiments – the 370th, the 371st, and the 372nd Infantry – won the same honour. When the First World War ended on 11 November 1918, more than 5,000 black soldiers had been wounded and 750 killed.

Sadly, African-American veterans returning from the trenches were not welcomed home as conquering heroes, and their participation in the war did little to advance the cause of civil rights directly. In fact, a fearful wave of lynching and anti-black violence swept the nation. Afraid that the newly returned black soldiers would demand fair treatment as men and as citizens, hate-filled whites decided the time was right to stop them 'stepping out of their place'. Discharged African-American servicemen, some still in uniform, were among the victims of white mobs during race riots which took place in more than 20 cities across the United States during 1919–20. In Washington DC 39 white and black people were either killed or fatally wounded during vicious street fighting on 19–20 July 1919. Similar scenes occurred in other cities – such as Chicago, Illinois; Charleston, South Carolina; and Knoxville, Tennessee – foreshadowing the civil rights struggles later in the century.

Native Americans at war

When America entered the First World War, the remnants of the ancient Iroquois Confederation declared war on Germany because, as non-citizens, they regarded themselves as a separate entity from the United States. The enlistment of Native Americans into the armed forces was strongly promoted by General Hugh Scott, who had been impressed by the use of Indians as a junior officer in the Frontier Army during the 1890s. As a result higher authorities supported the idea, and over six thousand Native Americans volunteered in May 1917, while a similar number was conscripted thereafter. The majority of these went into the army, while about two thousand joined the navy. Those soldiers sent overseas took well to trench warfare and found themselves in the thick of the fighting.

A Choctaw called Joseph Oklahombi earned the Croix de Guerre after he discovered a group of 250 German soldiers having a meal in a high-walled cemetery. Blocking the gate, Oklahombi killed 79 of them and the rest surrendered. Because of the obscurity of their language, Oklahombi and 17 other Choctaws helped the American Expeditionary Force win several key battles in the

Meuse-Argonne campaign in France. At least one Choctaw man was placed in each field company headquarters. They handled military communications by field telephone, translated radio messages into the Choctaw language, and wrote field orders to be carried by runners between companies. The German army captured about one out of four messengers, but never deciphered the messages written in Choctaw.

Following the signing of the Armistice in November 1918, an Act of Congress dated 6 November 1919 provided that Native American soldiers and sailors who served in the recent war, and who had been honourably discharged, 'may be granted citizenship by courts of competent jurisdiction'. On 2 June 1924 Congress at last granted citizenship to all Native Americans.[2] However, the Indian Citizenship Act did not provide full protection under the Bill of Rights to Native Americans living under tribal governments, and several nations – including the Hopi and the Iroquois – declined citizenship in favour of retaining sovereign nationhood.

The Great Migration

The First World War initiated other changes on the American home front that permanently affected the lives of US citizens, both black and white. While defence production increased, the war stifled the flow of immigrant labour. Hence workers were urgently required in the North, and African Americans seized the opportunity to leave behind the Jim Crow laws, lynching, and oppressive economic conditions of the South. Known as the Great Migration, this represented the largest internal movement of people in American history, and brought about 1.25 million blacks to the industrial centres of the Northern and mid-western states before the Depression of 1929 stemmed its flow.

African-American newspapers such as the Chicago *Defender* and the *Ledger* published stories about successful black immigrants that did much to encourage the movement northwards. Copies of these journals were circulated throughout the rural South, and countless people solicited the help of the editorial staff in securing employment. One man wrote from Houston, Texas, on 30 April 1917:

> *Dear Sir:* wanted to leave the South and Go any Place where a man will be any thing Except a Ker [cur] . . . I am 30 years old and have Good Experience in Freight Handler and Can fill Position from Truck to Ag[en]t . . . would like Chicago or Philadelphia But I dont Care where so long as I Go where a man is a man.'[3]

Those who could not afford the cost of travel were sometimes loaned the money by prospective employers. Like the Exodusters a generation earlier, entire families or communities often trekked north together.

Parts of the South were severely depopulated by the Great Migration. Alabama, Georgia, North Carolina, South Carolina, and Virginia each lost more than 100,000 inhabitants by 1920. Meanwhile, the size of urban African-American communities increased dramatically. For example, the population of Detroit grew by 611 per cent between 1910 and 1930, while those of Chicago and

Cleveland grew by 148 and 307 per cent respectively during the same period. Despite racial animosity, poor working and living conditions, and a harsh winter climate, most of the migrants remained in the North. In 1910 the National Urban League was formed by an alliance of black conservatives (led by Dr George E. Haynes) and white philanthropists and social workers began to help black migrants find employment, housing, and education.

The Klan revived

The Ku Klux Klan experienced a revival during the years prior to the First World War. This was greatly stimulated by a Hollywood film epic called *Birth of a nation*, released in 1915. Directed by legendary film-maker David W. Griffith, and based on the Reverend Thomas Dixon Jr's anti-black play *The clansman*, it featured columns of 'heroic' hooded Klansmen galloping through the night to save white civilisation, while blacks were portrayed as lazy, violent criminals who craved white women. Such powerful images were greeted enthusiastically by white supremacists. On Thanksgiving Night in 1915, 25,000 Klansmen paraded through the streets of Atlanta, Georgia, to celebrate the opening of the film. The NAACP (see Chapter 5) denounced the film as 'the meanest vilification of the Negro race'. Riots broke out in major cities, and subsequent law-suits and picketing activities followed the film for years. When Griffith, the son of a Confederate soldier, presented his work to Woodrow Wilson during a private screening in the White House, the president allegedly declared: 'It is like writing history with lightning. And my only regret is that it is all so terribly true.' To his credit, Griffith later released a shortened version of the film without references to the Klan, but the damage had been done.

The revived Klan was organised as a patriotic, Protestant fraternal society by William J. Simmons, a practising physician and defrocked minister of the Methodist Episcopal Church. This new Klan not only was anti-black, but directed its activities against any group it considered un-American, including immigrants, Jews, and Roman Catholics. Simmons introduced the symbol of the burning cross during his first appearance as imperial wizard, at Stone Mountain, Georgia, on Thanksgiving Day of 1915. Following the First World War Klan membership grew rapidly in both the North and the mid west as well as in the South, until by 1921 it claimed to have more than 100,000 members. Hiram Wesley Evans became the Klan's leader during the following year, and membership peaked at about four million in 1924. During the presidential campaign of 1928 the Klan started a hate campaign against the Democratic candidate, Albert E. Smith, because he was a Catholic. As a consequence, the Republican Herbert Hoover won the election.

Interest in the Klan waned dramatically during the late 1920s, and membership fell to only 45,000. This was mainly because of changing public perceptions following shocking revelations about criminality and corruption within the organisation. Furthermore, state laws forbade the wearing of masks and clamped down on the secret rituals practised during Klan gatherings.

The inter-war period

Roosevelt and civil rights

The roots of twentieth-century civil rights legislation may be found in the New Deal years of President Franklin D. Roosevelt. Prior to the stock market crash in 1929, and the Great Depression that followed, the vast majority of African Americans voted for the Republican Party – the party of Abraham Lincoln, the 'Great Emancipator'. In the 1932 presidential election – during the depths of the Depression, when about one-third of all black males were unemployed – the incumbent Republican president, Herbert Hoover, received more than three-quarters of the black vote over the Democratic candidate, Franklin D. Roosevelt.

However, Roosevelt won the election and went on to introduce a broad programme of economic reforms known as the New Deal. The economic benefits of the New Deal were distributed more or less equally to blacks and whites, and by January 1935 more than three million blacks, one-fifth of the black labour force, were employed on relief projects begun by the Federal government. During the 1936 presidential election millions of black voters were sufficiently impressed by Roosevelt and his New Deal economic programmes to switch from the Republicans to the Democrats.

In 1938 Roosevelt passed an executive order creating the Civil Rights Section of the Justice Department. Known subsequently as the Civil Rights Division, this provided a government agency to aid Southern blacks in their efforts to gain integration. Although it started slowly, the Civil Rights Section began to build a skilled bureaucracy of lawyers and other trained professionals to further the cause of black civil rights in the United States. In its early days the Civil Rights Section devoted itself to fighting for the right of blacks to vote in national elections and to opposing police brutality to blacks. Later it became an ally of the NAACP in filing suits to bring about school integration and in lobbying Congress to pass civil rights laws.

For example, in 1938 in *Missouri ex rel. Gaines v. Canada*, the Supreme Court took up the question of whether 'separate' black facilities were indeed 'equal' to those provided for whites. The facility in question was the whites-only law school at the University of Missouri. As the state did not have an equivalent institution for blacks, the court ruled that a black student named Lloyd Gaines should be permitted to attend the University of Missouri Law School. In stark contrast to the ruling in the case of *Cumming v. Board of Education* of 1899, this decision represented a major step forward in the cause of black civil rights. Anywhere that it could be shown that segregated facilities were not equal in quality, a suit could now be filed.

None the less, during the New Deal years the Democratic Party found it best to retain black votes by providing economic benefits rather than by advancing the cause of civil rights. Roosevelt had been elected by an uneasy coalition of Northern liberal voters, both black and white, and all-white Southern Democratic voters. This so-called 'Roosevelt Coalition' was strengthened by economic programmes that simultaneously aided Southern whites and Northern blacks. However, it was divided over the issue of civil rights, which appealed strongly to Northern Democrats but stirred inflamed opposition from segregation-oriented Southern Democrats. Influenced by issues of inequality brought to the nation's attention as a result of America's role in both the Second World War and the Cold War, civil rights would become a major political issue by the late 1940s.

The Second World War

The rise of fascism in Europe, with its racist and anti-Semitic policies, was of grave concern to many African Americans during the 1930s. The Italian invasion of the ancient empire of Abyssinia in north-east Africa during 1935 elicited a wave of protest from black civil rights leaders in America. But with the outbreak of general war in Europe following the German invasion of Poland, a neutral United States was unprepared for war.

Once again black Americans faced a particular dilemma. A strong desire to stamp out fascism was tempered by the experience of oppression and discrimination at home. Their dilemma was solved with the realisation that the war provided blacks with another opportunity to link military service to improvement in social justice in America. Insisting that their support for the war effort hinged on America's commitment to racial justice within its own borders, they made their feelings clear in the 'Double-V' campaign. Begun by the editors of the Pittsburgh newspaper *The Courier* on 7 February 1942, and later led by labour activist Asa Philip Randolph, this emphasised double victory: abroad against dictatorship, and at home against racial inequality and segregation. While the nation prepared for war, Randolph threatened to lead a march of 50,000 blacks on Washington DC to force President Franklin D. Roosevelt to end discrimination in government and the defence industries. Claiming to support a war for freedom and self-determination, Roosevelt succumbed and signed Executive Order 8802 on 25 June 1941. The first presidential directive on race since Reconstruction, this prohibited discriminatory employment practices by Federal agencies plus all unions and companies engaged in war-related work. Controlled by the Fair Employment Practice Commission (FEPC), which was made permanent in 1945 by President Harry Truman, this initiative unfortunately lacked effective enforcement powers and received inadequate Federal funding.

During the years 1942 and 1945 the proportion of blacks involved in war production increased from 3 to 9 per cent. Booming war production and a white labour force depleted by military conscription, or the draft, resulted in the employment of approximately 2 million African Americans in industry, plus a further 200,000 in the Federal civil service. By the end of the war, the black membership in labour unions had doubled to 1,250,000, while the number of skilled and semi-skilled black workers had nearly tripled. Membership of the NAACP also reached an all-time peak, rising from 50,000 to 450,000. A 1943 NAACP report indicated that race had become 'a global instead of a national or sectional issue'.[4]

Black activists also campaigned for impartial administration of the new conscription law, which resulted in more than three million African Americans being registered for military service under the Selective Service and Training Act of 1940. By the end of 1944, when the US Army was at its peak strength, it contained 701,678 blacks and had ended its non-combatant policy for these soldiers. The navy included 165,000 blacks and no longer restricted them to duty as officers' stewards. Furthermore, African Americans had ceased to be excluded from the Marine Corps and Coast Guard; these branches of service contained 17,000 and 5,000 blacks respectively by the end of the war.

In 1940 the black Federal judge William Hastie was appointed civilian aide to Secretary of War Cordell Hull, to assist with the rising number of African Americans in the armed forces. Hastie used his position to fight segregation and agitate for equal opportunities for black servicemen. In partial response, the War Department began training African Americans as aviation pilots at Tuskegee, Alabama, within a segregated unit; 450 of the Tuskegee airmen gained widespread recognition for their performance in the air war in the skies over north Africa, Sicily, and Europe.

Twenty-two black US Army combat units fought in the European theatre of the war, but all of these were segregated. The 761st Tank Battalion helped stem the German counter-attack during the Battle of the Bulge in December 1944. At the same time, the US Army appealed for volunteers among those soldiers serving in non-combat or service units behind the lines. Fighting side by side with white troops, the 2,500 blacks who volunteered to halt the Nazi attack were returned to their segregated units after the battle, and remained there until the end of the war. The black 371st Tank Battalion was the first allied force to liberate the Dachau and Buchenwald concentration camps in 1944. In the Pacific the black 24th Infantry took part in the assault on the New Georgia Islands during May 1942; and about 15,000 blacks from various units helped build the Burma Road, which linked Burma to China and provided Chinese forces with vital supplies needed to defeat the Japanese.

Document case study

Impact of war

6.1 An officer during the First World War recalls the conditions imposed on himself and other black soldiers by the US Army in France

Many of the field officers seemed far more concerned with reminding their Negro subordinates that they were Negroes than they were with having an effective unit that would perform well in combat. There was extreme concern lest the Negro soldiers be on too friendly terms with the French people. An infamous order from division headquarters . . . made speaking to a French woman a disciplinary offense . . . We were billeted in Joneville, Haute Marne, for a period of training, where the men moved freely among the populace. For no obvious reason we were moved out on the drill ground a quarter of a mile away and even the officers were forbidden to return to the village. When the townspeople came out on the following Sunday they found that the Negro soldiers had been prohibited from meeting and talking to them . . . One officer was put under arrest, guarded by a private with fixed bayonet, because the commanding officer saw him exchange a note with a French lady across the line . . .

Source: Howard H. Long, 'The negro soldier in the army of the United States', *Journal of Negro Education*, vol. 12 (summer 1943), pp. 311–12

6.2 Emmett J. Scott, special adjutant to the secretary of war, Newton D. Baker, on black involvement in the First World War in 1919

Intelligent Negroes . . . who got some idea of the real liberty in France although they were not permitted to enjoy it overmuch, are united in demanding better treatment from the American people and to this end have organized a League of Democracy to further their interest. They will not accept excuses, they say; they will not keep silence, they must be heard. They want to enjoy the same rights and privileges vouchsafed to all other citizens regardless of race, creed, or condition. Americans, therefore, they hope, will oppose those enemies to democracy at home that the Junkers [German ruling class] were to democracy in Europe. There must come a new day, Negroes feel, for the United States when the country will square itself with its own conscience and with the world in regard to its attitude toward the Negroes in America.

It will be interesting, therefore, to understand exactly what some of the colored leaders are thinking. A very advanced position has been taken by Dr. A. A. Graham, of Phoebus, Virginia, whose words may be quoted here:

'It is necessary now as never before that the black man press his claims as an American citizen. He should demand every right which this government owes to those who maintain its life and defend its honor. He should be willing to make no compromise of any kind, nor be satisfied with anything less than full justice. He has paid the price which all men have had to pay for liberty within the law. He has made the supreme sacrifice which entitled men to every just consideration of the government to which they pay allegiance. His shortcomings as a man and a human being did not excuse him from any of the duties and sacred responsibilities which the government imposed upon those whom it recognized as worthy of its claim upon them. He was called to volunteer when the country was in danger, as other men were called. He was conscripted. He was subjected to all the hard disciplines and exposures to death to which other men of the nation were exposed, and as an unquestioned American citizen, was asked to support all the war program from the purchase of savings stamps to the suffering and death in the trenches and on the battle field.'

Source: Emmett J. Scott, *Scott's official history of the American negro in the world war*, Chicago: Homewood Press, 1919, pp. 465–66

6.3 Account by a black university student in Chicago in 1920, who left the factory where he was working, unaware that a riot was in progress, and was attacked by about 20 men as he boarded a streetcar

The motorman opened the door, and before they knew it I jumped out and ran up Fifty-first Street as fast as my feet could carry me. Gaining about thirty yards [27 metres] on them was a decided advantage, for one of them saw me and with the shout 'There he goes!' the gang started after me. One, two, three, blocks went past in rapid succession. They came on shouting, 'Stop him! Stop him!' I ran on the sidewalk and someone tried to trip me, but fortunately I anticipated his intentions and jumped into the road . . . My strength was fast failing; the suggestion came into my mind to stop and give up or try to fight it out with the two or three who were still chasing me, but this would never do, as the odds were too great, so I kept on. My legs began to wobble, my breath came harder, and my heart seemed to be pounding like a big pump, while the man nearest me began to creep up on me. It was then that an old athletic maxim came into my mind—'He's feeling as tired as you.' Besides, I thought, perhaps he smokes and boozes and his wind is worse than mine. Often in the last hundred yards of a quarter-mile that thought of my opponent's condition had brought forth the last efforts necessary for the final spurt. There was more than a medal at stake this time, so I stuck, and in a few strides more they gave up the chase . . .

This is no place for a minister's son, I thought, and crept behind a fence and lay down among some weeds . . . Then the injustice of the whole thing overwhelmed me— emotions ran riot. Had the ten months I spent in France been all in vain? Were those little white crosses over the dead bodies of those dark-skinned boys lying in Flanders fields for naught? Was democracy merely a hollow sentiment? What had I done to deserve such treatment? I lay there experiencing all the emotions I imagined the innocent victim of a southern mob must feel when being hunted for some supposed crime. Was this what I had given up my Canadian citizenship for, to become an American citizen and soldier? Was the risk of a life in a country where such hatred existed worth while? Must a Negro always suffer merely because of the color of his skin?

Source: Chicago Commission on Race Relations, *The negro in Chicago, a study of race relations and a race riot*, Chicago: The University of Chicago Press, 1922, pp. 481–83

6.4 Letter in the Chicago newspaper *The Defender* in response to its many advertisements of jobs in the North

Lutcher, LA., May 13, 1917

Dear Sir: I have been reading the Chicago defender and seeing so many advertisements about the work in the north I thought to write you concerning my condition. I am working hard in the south and can hardly earn a living. I have a wife and one child and can hardly feed them. I thought to write and ask you for some information concerning how to get a pass for myself and family. I dont want to leave my family behind as I cant hardly make a living for them right here with them and I know they would fare hard if I would leave them. If there are any agents in the south there havent been any of them to Lutcher if they would come here they would get at least fifty men. Please sir let me hear from you as quick as possible. Now this is all. Please dont publish my letter, I was out in town today talking to some of the men and they say if they could get passes that 30 or 40 of them would come. But they havent got the money and they dont know how to come. But they are good strong and able working men. If you will instruct me I will instruct the other men how to come as they all want to work. Please dont publish this because we have to whisper this around among our selves because the white folks are angry now because the negroes are going north.

Source: Emmett J. Scott, 'Letters of negro migrants of 1916–1918,' *Journal of Negro History*, vol. 4 (July 1919), pp. 177–80

6.5 'Grand Wizard' Hiram Wesley Evans explains the beliefs of the Ku Klux Klan

There are three . . . great racial instincts, vital elements in both the historic and the present attempts to build an America which shall fulfil the aspirations and justify the heroism of the men who made the nation. These are the instincts of loyalty to the white race, to the traditions of America, and to the spirit of Protestantism, which has been an essential part of Americanism ever since the days of Roanoke and Plymouth Rock. They are condensed into the Klan slogan: 'Native, white, Protestant supremacy'.

Source: Hiram Wesley Evans, *The Klan's fight for 'Americanism'* (reprint from the *North American Review*, March 1926), Collection of Michigan State University

6.6 Report from the Paris edition of a US Army magazine on the mixing of black and white soldiers during the Battle of the Bulge

Negro doughboys are participating in the eastward sweep by General Hodges' force . . .

If comments of white personnel of these divisions are any indication, the plan of mixing white and colored troops in fighting units, a departure from previous United States Army practice, is operating successfully.

Negro reinforcements reported a sincere, friendly welcome everywhere. They also spoke of excellent relations with their white fellow doughs, of the making of inter-racial friendships.

The integration of the Negro platoons into their units was accomplished quickly and quietly. There was no problem . . .

'I was damned glad to get those boys,' said the CO of K company, Capt. Wesley J. Simons, of Snow Hill, Md. 'They fit into our company like any other platoon, and they fight like hell. Maybe that's because they were all volunteers and wanted to get into this.'

Source: Alan Morrison, *Stars and Stripes*, Paris edition, 6 April 1945

1 What insights does Document 6.1 provide into relationships between black and white soldiers during the First World War?

2 According to Documents 6.2 and 6.3, to what extent was the struggle for civil rights affected by the First World War?

3 How does Document 6.4 convey the plight of Southern blacks during the Great Migration?

4 Account for the changing policies of the revived Ku Klux Klan, as outlined in Document 6.5.

5 What impact might the mixing of white and black troops during the Battle of the Bulge, reported in Document 6.6, have had on racial integration in the United States?

Notes and references

1 Jonathan Earle, *The Routledge atlas of African American history*, New York, 2000, p. 82.

2 *US statutes at large*, Washington DC: US Government Printing Office, 1924, vol. 43, chapter 233, p. 253.

3 Emmett J. Scott, 'Letters of negro migrants of 1916–1918', *Journal of Negro History* (July 1919), p. 179.

4 Mary L. Dudziak, *Cold War civil rights*, Princeton, New Jersey, 2000, p. 9.

7 Civil rights in the Cold War

The motive for social reform

In recent years, historians such as Mary L. Dudziak have argued that the fight against communism during the post-1945 Cold War years forced American leaders to introduce key social reforms, including desegregation, because they were embarrassed on the world stage by oppressive race relations at home. As the 'presumptive leader of the free world', Dudziak claimed, 'how could American democracy be a beacon during the Cold War, and a model for those struggling against Soviet oppression, if the United States itself practised brutal discrimination against minorities within its own borders?'[1] Thus, a need for improved race relations in the United States, in order to uphold the principle of democracy abroad, was a major reason for the enactment of various civil rights initiatives during the presidencies of Harry S. Truman, John F. Kennedy, and Lyndon Baines Johnson.

Truman and civil rights

President Harry S. Truman was elected to office in his own right in 1948, having acceded to the presidency after the death of Franklin D. Roosevelt three years earlier. Succumbing to both internal and international pressure for reform, Truman met with the National Emergency Committee against Mob Violence on 19 September 1946. Composed of civil rights, religious, and labour groups, this body urged the president to act on widespread reports of violent racial abuse of blacks – such as the murder of ex-serviceman George Dorsey, plus his wife and two friends, in Georgia on 25 July 1946. As a result Truman authorised the establishment of a committee on civil rights to investigate the state of race relations in America.

On 29 October 1947 this body issued its landmark report *To secure these rights*, which offered three main reasons why civil rights abuses should be redressed in the United States: on moral grounds – it stated that discrimination was morally wrong; on economic grounds – discrimination harmed the economy; and on international grounds – discrimination damaged US foreign relations. Regarding the third of these, it commented: 'our domestic civil rights shortcomings are a serious obstacle'.[2] The report went on to make over 35 recommendations for action. These included demands for a Federal anti-lynching law, an expansion of the Civil Rights Section of the Justice Department, and the establishment of a permanent fair employment practices commission. Other recommendations called for an end to segregation on interstate transport, the abolition of segregated public schooling in the District of Columbia, and an end to discrimination and segregation in the armed forces.

In reality, there was little immediate likelihood of the committee's main proposals winning the congressional approval necessary for implementation. None the less, the focus on race relations was maintained during the 1948 presidential election campaign. Opinion polls indicated that Truman was lagging well behind the Republican challenger, Thomas Dewey. In contrast, Progressive Party candidate Henry Wallace, who was known for his commitment to civil rights, was capturing the white liberal and African-American votes. As a consequence, Clark Clifford, Truman's campaign manager, made black civil rights a major election issue. On 26 July 1948 Truman issued Executive Order 9981, designed to bring an end to segregation in the armed forces, and reinforced his commitment to civil rights. The Democrats secured a narrow electoral victory that led to further divisions within the party ranks, but placed Truman back in the White House for a second term.

Brown v. Board of Education

In 1950 the United States Information Agency published a pamphlet called *The negro in American life*, which contained a photograph captioned: 'In New York, a Negro teacher teaches pupils of both races.' By publishing and distributing such material, the Federal government was attempting to create the impression, at least on the international scene, that American democracy was a model for the world, and that its public schools had been desegregated. In fact the first steps towards desegregation in education were not taken until December 1952, when President Truman ordered the Justice Department to join the battle against Jim Crow in the case *Brown v. Board of Education of Topeka, Kansas*.

In Topeka, Kansas, an African-American third-grade student named Linda Brown had to walk one mile through a railroad switchyard to get to her all-black elementary school, even though a white elementary school was only seven blocks away from where she lived. Linda's father, Oliver Brown, tried to enrol his daughter in the nearby school, but the principal refused to accept her. Brown went to McKinley Burnett, the head of Topeka's branch of the NAACP, and asked for help. The NAACP had long wanted to challenge segregation in public schools and were eager to assist the Browns. In 1953 Thurgood Marshall of the NAACP Legal Defense Fund brought the matter before the Supreme Court.

Aware that the United States needed a response to Soviet anti-American propaganda, Chief Justice Earl Warren ruled on 17 May 1954 that separating white and coloured children in public schools had 'a detrimental effect upon the colored children. The impact is greater when it has the sanction of the law; for the policy of separating the races is usually interpreted as denoting the inferiority of the negro group.'[3]

When handed down by Chief Justice Warren, this landmark decision called for the desegregation of all public school systems throughout the nation 'with all deliberate speed'. The court unanimously ruled that separate facilities were, by definition, unequal and, therefore, unconstitutional. Most important, however, was the breadth of the decision. In outlawing segregation in *all* public education throughout the entire nation, the court implied that *all* forms of segregation were illegal. It could now be assumed that the court would uphold new civil rights legislation banning any form of public discrimination – provided, of course, that Congress could be persuaded to pass such laws.

Within a year of the 1954 decision, over five hundred school districts in the North and the Upper South had quietly desegregated. But in the Deep South open and complete defiance began as soon as the Supreme Court finding was announced. Herman Talmadge, the governor of Georgia, declared that his state would 'not tolerate the mixing of the races in the public schools or any other tax-supported institutions'. In many Southern townships white citizens' councils were formed to combat school integration by threatening loss of business to persons employing those who supported compliance with the court decision. Meanwhile, the Ku Klux Klan maintained a campaign of terror and violence against anyone who supported desegregation.

In March 1956 a 'Southern manifesto' was issued by 96 Southern Congressmen. It denounced the *Brown* ruling and called for 'all lawful means to bring about a reversal of this decision which is contrary to the Constitution'.[4] The pace of integration began to slow down considerably.

Black initiatives

Little Rock

The next important test of the determination of the Federal government to back integration occurred in September 1957, when Orval Faubus, governor of Arkansas, blocked a Federal court order directing the Central High School in Little Rock to admit nine qualified African-American students. Faubus threatened violence if the nine attempted to gain access, and called out the National Guard to 'monitor' the school.

When the nine black students tried to enrol at the school on 3 September, the National Guardsmen prevented them from entering the building, while a large crowd of segregationists jeered and threatened to lynch them. Ten days later, in a meeting with President Dwight D. Eisenhower, Faubus agreed to use the National Guard to protect the African-American teenagers; but on returning to Little Rock he dismissed the troops, leaving the black students exposed to an angry white mob. Within hours the jeering, brick-throwing mob had beaten several reporters and smashed many of the school's windows and doors. By noon local police were forced to evacuate the nine students. When Faubus failed to restore order, President Eisenhower put the Arkansas National Guard under Federal command and dispatched a thousand paratroopers from the 101st Airborne Division to

A jeering student follows Elizabeth Eckford as she walks down a line of National Guardsmen who barred her from entering the Little Rock Central High School on 3 September 1957.

Little Rock. By 3 a.m., the school was surrounded by soldiers with fixed bayonets, and the students were escorted in to school that day.

Although they suffered physical violence and constant racial abuse, the 'Little Rock Nine' completed the school year – but parents of four of them lost their jobs because they had insisted on sending their children to a white school. On 27 May 1958 one of the 'Nine', Ernest Green, joined six hundred senior classmates in commencement ceremonies at Quigley Stadium, and became the first black student to graduate from Little Rock Central High. Federal troops and city police were on hand but the event went peacefully. The following month Federal District Judge Harry Lemley granted a delay on further integration at the school until January 1961, stating that while black students had a constitutional right to attend white schools the time had not come for them 'to enjoy that right'. The NAACP appealed unsuccessfully.

During August 1958 Governor Faubus called a special session of the state legislature to pass a law allowing him to close public schools to avoid integration and to lease the closed schools to private school corporations. On 12 September the Supreme Court ruled that Little Rock must continue with its integration plan, following which the school board announced that the city's high schools would open on 15 September. Faubus next ordered Little Rock's three high schools to be closed. As a result, the city's 3,698 high-school students were forced to seek alternatives. More than 750 whites enrolled in the newly established private T. J. Raney High School. Others left town or the state to live with friends or relatives to continue their education.

Finally, on 18 June 1959, the Federal court declared that the state of Arkansas school-closing law was unconstitutional, and the public high schools were reopened on an integrated basis during the autumn of that year. However, as the 1950s drew to a close, fewer than 1 per cent of black students in the Deep South were enrolled in desegregated schools.

Congress of Racial Equality

The Congress of Racial Equality (CORE) had been founded as the Committee of Racial Equality by an inter-racial group of students at the University of Chicago during June 1942. Initially co-led by white student George Houser, plus black students James Farmer and Bayard Rustin, many of these young campaigners were members of the Chicago branch of the Fellowship of Reconciliation (FOR), a pacifist organisation seeking to change racist attitudes. Deeply influenced by the Indian nationalist leader Mahatma Gandhi's teachings of non-violent resistance, CORE sought to integrate restaurants, snack bars, lunch counters, and public rest rooms throughout the North, the border states, and the Upper South. Expanding its membership during the mid 1940s, CORE established local chapters throughout the North. Farmer became its first national director in 1943.

CORE's preferred methods of demonstration were the 'freedom ride' and the 'sit-in'. In April 1947 the organisation sent eight white and eight black men on a two-week pilgrimage through Virginia, North Carolina, Tennessee, and Kentucky to test a Supreme Court ruling that declared segregation in interstate travel unconstitutional. Dubbed the 'Journey of Reconciliation', this action gained national attention when four of the riders were arrested at Chapel Hill, North Carolina, and three – including Bayard Rustin – were sentenced to thirty days on a chain gang.

The Journey of Reconciliation achieved a great deal of publicity and was the start of a long campaign of direct action by CORE. In February 1948 the Council against Intolerance in America gave Houser and Bayard Rustin the Thomas Jefferson Award for the Advancement of Democracy for their attempts to bring an end to segregation in interstate travel.

Montgomery bus boycott

Although blacks and whites were permitted to travel in the same city buses in Montgomery, Alabama, the seating had been racially segregated since the introduction of the Jim Crow laws. Whites sat at the front of the bus, filling seats progressively towards the rear. Blacks were to sit at the back of the bus and occupied seats progressively towards the front. If the bus was so crowded that a white person had to stand, a black passenger was required by Montgomery municipal law to give up their seat to the white person.

After a tiring day at work on 1 December 1955, Mrs Rosa Parks, a black seamstress, boarded a city bus and sat in the first row of seats in the black section of the bus. When a white man got on the bus, driver James F. Blake ordered Mrs Parks to give up her seat and move back. She refused to move, and Blake called the police to have her arrested.

Rosa Parks was subsequently released on bail paid by E. D. Nixon, the Montgomery representative of the Brotherhood of Sleeping Car Porters and a local leader of the NAACP. During the next few days, it occurred to Nixon that Montgomery's black citizens might demonstrate their disapproval of the city's segregated bus system. He met with the Reverends Ralph Abernathy and Martin Luther King Jr, plus Jo Ann Robinson, the leader of a black women's group known as the Women's Political Council. It was decided that a bus boycott was the best way to respond to the arrest of Rosa Parks.

Forty thousand handbills were printed and distributed among the members of the black community of Montgomery. Furthermore, on 4 December black ministers throughout the city conveyed the message from their pulpits. The boycott began on Monday 5 December, and it was an immediate success.

At the end of the first day of action, during which 90 per cent of the city's 40,000 blacks stayed off the buses, Martin Luther King Jr was elected to lead the campaign. Ironically, Dr King had been considered a safe choice when appointed minister of the Dexter Avenue Baptist Church in 1952. He replaced the Reverend Vernon Johns, who had been campaigning against segregated city buses in Montgomery since 1948.

The bus boycott continued for over a year. Many blacks walked to their destinations, while others rode in car pools or received free automobile rides from volunteer drivers supporting the cause. The bus company lost about 65 per cent of its business and had to cut services, lay off drivers, and raise fares.

After the boycott had been underway for about 80 days, a desperate Montgomery municipal administration ordered the arrest of Dr King and a hundred other black leaders. In a packed meeting the same day, King pointed out that the conflict was not 'between the white and the Negro', but between 'justice and injustice'. Embracing the philosophical commitment to non-violent direct action promoted by CORE during the 1940s, he urged his followers to love rather than hate those who opposed them.

The bus boycott continued until final victory was achieved in November 1956, when the Supreme Court ruled that the Montgomery bus company's policy of segregation violated the US Constitution. In response, the company agreed not only to end segregation on their vehicles, but also to hire black drivers. Bus passengers were to be integrated on 21 December 1956. Black church leaders advised their members to sit where they wished on the bus on that day, but not to retaliate in response to violence. At 5.55 that morning, Dr King and the Reverend Glen Smiley, a white friend, boarded a bus, paid their fares, sat together at the front of the vehicle, and made a historic journey. The city of Montgomery, Alabama, had produced the most important leader of the civil rights movement; and non-violent demonstration, the most effective weapon of protest, had made its first massive contribution to the struggle for racial equality in the United States.

Student sit-ins

One of the most obvious forms of racial discrimination in the late 1950s and early 1960s was the refusal of snack bars, lunch counters, and restaurants to serve African Americans. On 1 February 1960 four black college students – Franklin McCain, Joseph McNeil, Ezell Blair Jr, and David Richmond – successfully staged a sit-in at the lunch counter in the Woolworth store on South Elm Street in Greensboro, North Carolina. Although CORE had used sit-ins to oppose racial segregation publicly since the early 1940s, this particular sit-in, perhaps because it involved college students, received extensive coverage in the national news media, particularly on network television.

All at once students at other black colleges throughout the South began to stage sit-ins in an effort to end racial segregation in nearby eating-houses. Students at white colleges often joined these sit-ins, as did sympathetic high-school students and adults of both races. Frequently these demonstrations resulted in violence, with white segregationists taunting and beating up the demonstrators, thereby producing even more coverage by the news media. By January 1961, as Eisenhower was leaving office, over 70,000 black and white youngsters had participated in sit-ins. A new civil rights organisation, the Student Non-violent Co-ordinating Committee (SNCC), was formed on 16–17 April 1960, initially to organise sit-in demonstrations throughout the South.

Following in the footsteps of CORE, SNCC members adopted the Gandhian approach of non-violent direct action. Their activities included participation in the freedom rides during 1961. Leading figures in the organisation included Robert Moses, Marion Barry, James Lawson, James Forman, and John Lewis, with Charles McDew as chairman. During 1963 John Lewis replaced McDew as chairman and was one of the main speakers at the famous March on Washington on 28 August 1963.

Legislation

Civil Rights Acts, 1957 and 1960

President Eisenhower's second term in office saw the passage of the 1957 and 1960 Civil Rights Acts. Although privately opposed to integration, Eisenhower had felt publicly obliged to support the *Brown* decision on education, because of ongoing concerns about America's standing on the international scene. During the 1956 presidential election, he ran for a second term in office with a platform that included measures designed to win the white liberal vote. Once back in the White House, he authorised the Senate majority leader Lyndon Baines Johnson to steer the Civil Rights Act of 1957 through the Senate. Although it had to be watered down considerably, this Act represented the first civil rights legislation for 82 years, and it empowered the Justice Department to initiate law-suits in voting rights cases. It also established the bipartisan Civil Rights Commission to investigate violations of the law. The resolve of Southern white politicians stiffened with the passage of this legislation, and white segregationists continued to prevent blacks from voting wherever possible by making it virtually impossible for blacks to register their vote.

The 1960 Civil Rights Act only slightly strengthened the enforcement provisions of the first measure. This provided for the enrolment of qualified blacks by voting referees appointed by Federal district court judges, in areas where local registrars had denied such persons the right to vote. Voting records were also to be preserved for 22 months and subject to Federal inspection. The African-American community was divided with regard to both Acts. Martin Luther King Jr and Roy Wilkins, executive secretary of the NAACP since 1955, gave only lukewarm support. CORE leader Bayard Rustin believed that the passage of both Acts implied a new attitude on the part of the Federal government, and that they would further encourage blacks to fight for their rights.

Kennedy and civil rights

The civil rights record of President John F. Kennedy is mixed. During his election campaign he made a strong commitment to the cause by promising, if elected, to end discrimination in Federal housing provision 'with the stroke of a pen'. During October 1960, less than one month before the nation went to the polls, Martin Luther King Jr was given a four-month jail sentence for participation in a sit-in protest in Atlanta, Georgia. While Kennedy's Republican opponent, Richard Nixon, remained aloof, Kennedy responded with a personal phone call to Coretta Scott, King's wife, to assure her of his support. Furthermore, the candidate's brother, Robert Kennedy, used his influence to persuade the Georgia state judge involved in the case to authorise King's release from prison the following day. As a result Kennedy gained 75 per cent of the African-American vote, helping him to achieve a narrow victory in one of the most tightly contested presidential elections of the twentieth century.

Once in office, Kennedy appointed over 40 blacks to important positions in government. Among these, the NAACP lawyer Thurgood Marshall was made a US circuit court judge. Robert C. Weaver was given responsibility for the Housing and Home Finance Agency, and journalist Carl Rowan was made assistant secretary of state. A white lawyer, Harris Wofford, was appointed special assistant to the president on civil rights. Kennedy also sent troops to Oxford, Mississippi, in 1962 to enforce a court order directing the all-white state university to admit black student James Meredith. In the violence that ensued, two people were killed, including a French reporter, and hundreds were wounded. The violence in Oxford, and the Federal role in managing the crisis, did not go unnoticed abroad.

However, Kennedy was reluctant to propose a civil rights bill, or even to support one drafted by the liberals in Congress, for fear of jeopardising other aspects of his New Frontier reform programme. He believed that executive action could achieve more for blacks than legislation. Hence during April 1961 he had authorised presidential Executive Order 10925, which provided for improved employment opportunities for blacks in the Federal government. Finally, on 20 November 1962, he fulfilled his campaign pledge to end segregation in Federal housing via Executive Order 11063. Not passed as swiftly as he had promised, owing to his slim majority in Congress, this measure was also narrow in scope, applying only to new Federal construction projects, not to existing housing. Meanwhile, Attorney General Robert Kennedy felt less constrained, and vigorously employed litigation to hasten desegregation in schools and bus terminals. He also took action to expand black voting rights.

But black leaders remained unimpressed, pointing to the number of segregationists the president had appointed to judgeships in the South, and to his long delay in issuing Executive Order 11063. Indeed, Martin Luther King Jr accused him of having settled for 'token' progress in civil rights matters.

Birmingham protests

The Southern Christian Leadership Conference (SCLC) was formed in 1957 by Martin Luther King Jr, the Reverend Ralph Abernathy, Fred Shutterworth, and Bayard Rustin. The SCLC was based in Atlanta, Georgia. Its main objective was to co-ordinate and assist local organisations working for the full equality of African Americans. King was elected president and Abernathy secretary-treasurer. Committed to using non-violence in the struggle for civil rights, the SCLC adopted the motto 'Not one hair of one head of one person should be harmed.'

During April 1963 King and Shutterworth organised peaceful demonstrations in Birmingham, Alabama, a city that had the worst segregation record in the South. Imprisoned for involvement in a sit-in, King wrote his 'Letter from a Birmingham jail' in response to a public statement of 'concern and caution' issued by eight Southern white religious leaders. Released soon after, King – with his supporters – went ahead with a protest march on 3 May 1963. Composed mainly of African-American children and teenagers, the demonstration was planned by SCLC member James Bevel with the intention of filling the already overcrowded prisons with black youths, thereby embarrassing the Birmingham city officials.

Soon after the Birmingham march began, police chief Eugene 'Bull' Connor fell for the bait and countered the young protesters with fire hoses and police dogs. Televised images of children being water hosed, beaten, and arrested had a profound impact – not just on the American public, but on the rest of the world. During the days that followed, one-fifth of radio output in the Soviet Union was devoted to the subject, while newspaper headlines were typified by that published in Kenya: 'Riots Flare in U.S. South – Infants Sent to Jail'.

Concern about the international impact of the Birmingham riots led the Kennedy administration to send Assistant Attorney General Burke Marshall to the city to help manage negotiations that resulted in an agreement between the SCLC, the local government, and the business community. Under the terms of the pact, steps were to be taken within 90 days to integrate large department stores, while employment discrimination was to be redressed and civil rights demonstrators were to be released from jail.

An urgent need for positive Federal action presented itself again when Governor George Wallace stood in the school-house door to block the integration of the University of Alabama on 11 June 1963. On 21 May of that year, a Federal district judge had ordered the university to admit two black students, Vivian Malone and James Hood, to its summer session. In his inauguration speech earlier in the year, Wallace had pledged 'Segregation now! Segregation tomorrow! Segregation forever!' After careful intervention from Washington DC, and a direct order from the president to 'federalize' the Alabama National Guard to enforce the law, the students were quietly registered later the same day.

The fact that Kennedy could use 'federalized' state troops rather than paratroopers from the 101st Airborne Division, as deployed by President Eisenhower in 1957, was some indication of the progress made towards integration by this time. However, the need to respond further to the crisis in Alabama motivated President Kennedy to take a step both his advisers and civil rights activists had been urging for some time. On the evening of 11 June 1963 he addressed the nation on television and radio in a speech in which he identified the problem of racial disharmony as 'a moral issue . . . as old as the scriptures and . . . as clear as the American Constitution'. Mindful of the role of the United States on the international stage, he declared:

> Today we are committed to a worldwide struggle to promote and protect the rights of all who wish to be free. And when Americans are sent to Viet-Nam or West Berlin, we do not ask for whites only. It ought to be possible, therefore, for American students of any color to attend any public institution they select without having to be backed up by troops.[5]

Later that month, Kennedy placed the full weight of his administration behind a powerful piece of legislation that would become the Civil Rights Act of 1964.

March on Washington

The civil rights campaign continued to gather momentum during the summer of 1963. On 28 August 250,000 people marched peacefully to the Lincoln Memorial in Washington DC to demand equal justice for all citizens under the law. The march was organised by NAACP elder statesman A. Philip Randolph, who had suggested a similar march in 1941, and CORE leader Bayard Rustin. It was agreed with other labour and civil rights leaders that the specific aim of the March on Washington should be to demand the passage of a *meaningful* Civil Rights Act. They also sought the integration of public schools by the end of the year, and the enactment of a fair employment practices bill which would prohibit job discrimination, plus job training and placement.

In the wake of events in Alabama, Kennedy believed that the event in Washington would turn violent, and tried to persuade the civil rights leaders to call off the march. He also felt that such a demonstration might delay and perhaps destroy any possibility of a civil rights bill being passed. The president

Roy Wilkins (centre), executive secretary of the NAACP, and A. Philip Randolph (right), organiser of the demonstration, lead the March on Washington DC on 28 August 1963.

recommended that the campaigners should prove their peaceful intentions by staying off the streets. However, when he realised how determined the demonstration leaders were, he reluctantly endorsed the cause.

The theme of the march became racial harmony and unity, and demonstrators carried signs that read 'We march for integration'. Over 30 specially chartered 'Freedom Trains' and 2,000 'Freedom Buses' brought people to the capital from all over the nation. The hundred or so US senators and congressmen who attended the event were greeted with the chant 'Pass the bill – pass the bill'.

A. Philip Randolph was the first to speak. Standing on the steps of the Lincoln Memorial, he declared: 'Fellow Americans, we are gathered here in the largest demonstration in the history of this nation . . . We are the advance guard of a massive moral revolution for jobs and freedom.' Several of the speakers persuaded the people to step up their civil rights activities. Roy Wilkins, executive secretary of the NAACP, announced: 'You've got religion here today. Don't backslide tomorrow.' The hardest-hitting speech of the day came from John Lewis, leader of the SNCC, who declared: 'By the force of our demands, our determination and our numbers, we shall splinter the segregated South into a thousand pieces, and put them back together in the image of God and Democracy.'

Then Martin Luther King Jr stepped up to the microphone. The most popular of all the civil rights leaders, he delivered a speech of hope and determination which epitomised the day's message of racial harmony, love, and a belief that blacks and whites could live together in peace. Known subsequently as the 'I have a dream' speech, it included one of the black leader's most potent statements: 'I have a dream that my four children will one day live in a nation where they will not be judged by the color of their skin but by the content of their character.'[6]

Receiving worldwide media coverage, the March on Washington was a resounding success. Contrary to expectations, there were no major disturbances, and the two thousand National Guard on hand were not necessary. Instead, millions of Americans witnessed for the first time black and white people united in the cause of freedom and civil rights for all. In Europe, according to the US Information Agency, 'most comment found the Washington March a ringing affirmation of the power of the American democratic process'. In Ghana, on the African continent, the *Evening News* called the march one of the 'greatest revolutions in the annals of human history'.

The positive news coverage was short lived. On 15 September 1963 a bomb exploded in the Sixteenth Street Baptist Church in Birmingham, Alabama, killing four young girls as they prepared for Sunday school. This was followed by the assassination of John F. Kennedy in Dallas, Texas, on 22 November 1963. The progress of civil rights in America was temporarily stopped in its tracks.

Freedom Summer

The civil rights activists were not subdued for long. In 1964 the SNCC joined with CORE and the NAACP to organise the 'Freedom Summer' campaign. The main objective of this coalition, called the Mississippi Council of Federated Organizations, was to bring an end to the political disenfranchisement of African Americans in the Deep South. Volunteers from the three organisations agreed to concentrate their energies in Mississippi, where only 6.2 per cent of blacks were registered to vote in 1962. This was the lowest percentage in the nation.

Over 80,000 people joined the Mississippi Freedom Party and 68 delegates attended the Democratic Party Convention in Atlantic City, New Jersey, where they challenged the attendance of the all-white Mississippi representation. Hundreds of college students flocked south and joined with veteran civil rights activists to help with voter registration. The SNCC, CORE, and the NAACP also established 30 'freedom schools' in towns throughout Mississippi; there volunteers taught a curriculum that included black history and the philosophy of the civil rights movement. Over three thousand students attended these schools during the summer of 1964.

However, freedom schools were often targets of white mob violence. So also were the homes of local African Americans involved in the campaign. During the summer of 1964, 30 black homes and 37 black churches were firebombed, while more than 80 volunteers were attacked, either by white mobs or racist police officers. The most infamous act of violence was the murder of three young civil rights workers. On 21 June 1964 black volunteer James Chaney and white co-workers Andrew Goodman and Michael Schwerner set out to investigate a church bombing near Philadelphia, Mississippi. Arrested that afternoon, they were held for several hours on alleged traffic violations. Their release from jail was the last time they were seen alive; their badly decomposed bodies were discovered under a dam six weeks later. Goodman and Schwerner had died from single gunshot wounds to the chest, while Chaney had been beaten to death.

The Mississippi murders made headlines all over America, and provoked an outpouring of international support for the civil rights movement. But many black volunteers realised that, because two of the victims were white, these murders were attracting far more attention than previous attacks in which victims had been black, and this added to their growing resentment.

Johnson's 'Great Society'

Following the assassination of John F. Kennedy, the executive passed to Vice-President Lyndon Baines Johnson, of Texas. After serving out the remainder of Kennedy's term of office, Johnson was elected president in his own right during November 1964, and remained in the White House until January 1969.

Despite his Southern background, Johnson supported the campaign for civil rights more enthusiastically than either Eisenhower or Kennedy, and made over two hundred speeches with a civil rights theme. In his first State of the Union address, he described his vision of a 'Great Society' that would include a 'war on poverty', Federal support for education, medical care for the elderly, and legal protection for blacks deprived of voting rights by state regulations. He also proposed a new department of housing and urban development to co-ordinate Federal housing projects. Congress enacted almost all of these proposals, which represented the largest amount of legislation since the New Deal of the 1930s.

Initiated by John F. Kennedy in the wake of the riots in Birmingham, Alabama, during 1963, the Civil Rights Act of 1964 specifically prohibited racial discrimination in restaurants, snack bars, hotels, motels, swimming pools, and all other places of public accommodation throughout America. Via Title VI of this Act, funds could be withheld from any US government-supported school and/or education programme found practising racial discrimination. That year only two Southern states, Texas and Tennessee, had more than 2 per cent of their black students enrolled in integrated schools. The 1964 Act also established an equal opportunities commission to combat employment discrimination based on sex, religion, or race.

None the less, black disenfranchisement continued to be widespread. In Dallas County, Alabama, half the voting-age population was African American, but only 156 of 15,000 voting-age blacks were registered to vote by 1961. In spite of Justice Department efforts to use litigation to expand voting rights, by 1964 the number of African-American voters remained very low.

Voting Rights Act, 1965

As President Johnson approached the end of his first full year in office, he hoped to turn his attention to matters other than civil rights. He informed Martin Luther King Jr that 1965 would not be the right time for a voting rights act. Such a measure would cost the president white Southern votes required for other Great Society programmes. But an attack on peaceful marchers in Alabama on 7 March 1965 focused the nation's attention on the extreme measures continually being used to prevent black citizens from exercising their constitutional right to vote. Intent on marching from Selma to Montgomery, civil rights activists got as far as the Edmund Pettus Bridge, over the Alabama River, when mounted state troopers attacked them with clubs and tear gas. The violence continued with the death in Birmingham of James Reed, a white clergyman from Boston who had gone to Alabama to support the civil rights movement. In response to the gathering outside the White House of over a thousand civil rights supporters on 13 March, Johnson told reporters: 'What happened in Selma was an American tragedy. The blows that were received, the blood that was shed, the life of the good man that was lost must strengthen the determination of each of us to bring full and equal and exact justice to all of our people.'[7]

The Selma March was a pivotal moment in the struggle for civil rights in the United States. In response to events during March 1965, Johnson appeared before a joint session of Congress and called for a voting rights act to be passed expeditiously. 'There is no Negro problem,' he declared. 'There is no Southern problem. There is no Northern problem. There is only an American problem.'

As a result, Johnson secured within six months the passage of the Voting Rights Act of 1965. This new law was designed to enforce the 15th Amendment of 1869. At one stroke, Section 4 of the Act abolished literacy tests, poll taxes, and all other devices used to discriminate against minority voters. The so-called heart of the Act was Section 5, which mandated that any change in election law, including something as small as moving a polling place, must be 'pre-cleared', or officially approved beforehand, either through the US Justice Department or through the Federal district court in the District of Columbia.

The number of African-American registered voters increased immediately after the signing of the Voting Rights Act (see map on p. 96). Within a year there were more than 230,000 new black voters throughout America, and the number continued to rise in subsequent decades. The most dramatic changes occurred in Florida, where black registration increased from 25 per cent in 1958 to over 50 per cent in 1965. By 1996 the Voting Rights Act had altered the face of American government. In 1965 the South had only 72 African-American elected officials; by 1976 there were 1,944. At the start of the twenty-first century there were nearly 5,000 – 68 times as many as when the Voting Rights Act was passed.

Vietnam

Meanwhile, the message of positive progress in domestic race relations promoted by the press and the US propaganda programme had succeeded in calming international criticism. Furthermore, concern with justice on the home

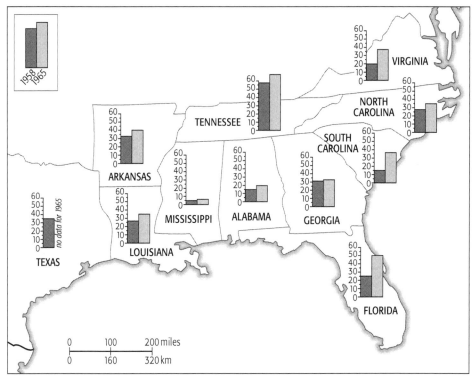

Black voters as a percentage of non-whites of voting age, 1958 and 1965 (adapted from J. Earle, *The Routledge atlas of African American history*, 2000, p. 112).

front was quickly replaced with a broad-based, worldwide condemnation of American militarism abroad. By 1966 the Vietnam War had replaced American race relations as the most important matter of international concern. The escalating American military situation in Vietnam did nothing to ease racial tension at home. When US forces were first committed to the fighting in Vietnam following the Gulf of Tonkin incident of August 1964, only regular soldiers were used. However, as the fighting escalated it was decided to use conscripts, or draftees, rather than to activate Reserve or National Guard units to meet troop needs. This resulted in a disproportionate number of blacks entering the armed forces; they constituted some 16 per cent of all those drafted, compared with 11 per cent of the national population called into military service. This was primarily owing to the inability of many blacks to receive deferments, plus their lack of representation on local draft boards.

From 1967 until his assassination the following year, Martin Luther King Jr condemned US involvement in Vietnam, which encouraged increasing numbers of blacks and liberal whites to oppose the conflict. At the war's end, black veterans who had fought as bravely as whites felt more keenly a sense of defeat when subjected to continued prejudice and rejection at home.

Black power

While President Johnson's civil rights legislation did much to help African Americans make substantial progress in the direction of equality, the gains served only to increase the frustration and bitterness among many blacks. This resulted from the fact that neither the right to vote nor legal guarantees of equality of opportunity did anything directly to improve their economic condition. Black unemployment remained twice the national average, with almost one-third of the black population living below the poverty line. Black schools and black housing remained inferior. While black purchasing power marginally increased, the economic gap between the two races continued to widen.

As a result, many young African Americans, particularly in the Northern ghettos, became greatly disillusioned with the aims and methods of the civil rights movement, which tended to become absorbed into a broader-based cacophony of protest for social change. This led to a shift away from the moderate approach of Martin Luther King Jr and the NAACP, towards black militancy.

Racial tension erupted into violence in America in August 1965, when some of the worst rioting since the 1860s broke out in the Watts district of Los Angeles, leaving 34 dead. The next two years were marked by riots in practically every major American city as blacks began shifting towards an independent course of action which came to be known as 'black nationalism' and 'black power'. These terms originated with a young West Indian named Stokely Carmichael who emigrated to the United States in 1952. After campaigning as a freedom rider and being heavily involved in the Freedom Summer project, Carmichael became the chairman of the SNCC in 1966. Becoming more militant, he dropped the word 'non-violent' from that group's name, and shortly afterwards ejected whites from its membership.

Other prominent militant organisations included the Black Muslims. This was a puritanical religious sect that rejected Christianity in favour of Islam, and preached that all whites were devils. Begun by Noble Drew Ali (born Timothy Drew) – who founded the organisation as the Moorish Science Temple in Newark, New Jersey, in 1913 – it was soon afterwards renamed the Nation of Islam. This group was taken over by Elijah Muhammad, alias Robert Poole, in 1934. By the 1960s it was unofficially known as the Black Muslims after the publication of a book by C. Eric Lincoln entitled *The black Muslims in America* (1961). Although the group numbered only about eight thousand when Muhammad took over, it grew rapidly in the 1950s and 1960s, particularly as a result of the preaching of one of its ministers, Malcolm X. However, tension grew between Muhammad and Malcolm X, and in 1964 the latter split from the Black Muslims to form the Organization of Afro-American Unity (OAAU). On 21 February 1965 Malcolm X was shot dead by three members of the Nation of Islam during a speaking engagement at the Audubon Ballroom in Manhattan. His death caused great dissension in the black nationalist movement.

The Black Panthers were a paramilitary group founded in Oakland, California, during October 1966 as a result of the assassination of Malcolm X, and subsequent to the urban uprising in Watts. Co-founded by Bobby Seale, who became the chairman, and Huey P. Newton, who was their minister of defence, the Black Panthers wanted to make African Americans aware that they had the right to carry guns. Their flamboyant display of firearms and their willingness to meet police brutality with force quickly made headlines from coast to coast. This organisation grew to at least five thousand members nationwide, and it was involved in numerous violent confrontations with the police. This tended to distract attention from some of their more philanthropic activities, such as the provision of food for black ghetto children and legal aid for the ghetto blacks.

Assassination of Martin Luther King Jr

During March 1968 Martin Luther King Jr travelled to Memphis, Tennessee, to support a labour strike among the all-black municipal sanitation workers. The strike, which had developed into a bitter conflict, was for union recognition, higher wages, fringe benefits, and safer working conditions. During a protest march led by King on 28 March, some of the demonstrators cast aside the non-violent principles he espoused and began breaking plate-glass windows and looting stores. The Memphis police force responded promptly and violently towards all the marchers. This was the first time King and his fellow organisers had lost control of a protest march. As the situation deteriorated, King's colleagues forced him to leave the march against his will in order to guarantee his personal safety.

On 3 April 1968 King addressed a black rally in Memphis supporting the sanitation strike, during which he made reference to his own mortality. He suggested that he might not live long enough to see the racial justice for which he and so many others had been working for so long. 'I may not get there with you,' he concluded, 'but we as a people will get to the promised land.'

King was killed the following evening by a bullet from a high-powered rifle as he stood on the balcony of his motel in Memphis. As the news spread throughout the nation, riots broke out in the African-American communities of more than 130 cities, including Washington DC. During seven days of rioting, 46 people were killed, all but 5 of whom were black. Some 2,600 fires were started that caused property damage of over $100 million. State governors had to call out the National Guard to quell the violence. President Johnson was forced to order in regular army troops in a number of larger cities. Over 20,000 rioters were arrested. It was the most concentrated week of racial violence the United States had ever known.

The Kerner Commission, 1968

The separation of blacks and whites in most areas was emphasised in March 1968 with the publication of the findings of the National Advisory Commission on Civil Disorder, or Kerner Commission. Established by President Johnson via

Executive Order 11365 on 29 July 1967, in response to the widespread urban riots that year, and headed by the Illinois state governor Otto Kerner, this report blamed the troubles on 'pervasive discrimination and segregation in employment, education and housing'. Advising that further strife could be avoided only by huge Federal government efforts to create jobs, improve education, and clear the slums, it concluded that the nation was 'moving towards two societies, one black, one white, separate and unequal'.

In response Johnson spurred Congress into passing the Fair Housing Act of 1968, which prohibited racial discrimination in the sale or letting of housing. But beyond that, nothing was done to implement the recommendations of the Kerner Commission.

None the less, real success had already been achieved in education. Black college students were enrolling in previously white colleges at a greater rate. In 1964, 51 per cent of black students had been in predominantly black colleges, but by 1971 only 34 per cent remained segregated. At the primary and secondary levels the South had begun to move ahead of the North. By the autumn of 1972, 44 per cent of black students in the South were in predominantly white schools, while only 30 per cent were in predominantly white schools in the North.

Nixon and civil rights

The civil rights movement received a major setback in 1970 when Republican President Richard Nixon announced that the integration of schools would be left to the courts and that his administration would downgrade strong desegregation procedures. On 20 April 1971 the Supreme Court ruled unanimously in *Swan v. Charlotte-Mecklenburg Board of Education* that the busing of students could be ordered to 'achieve racial desegregation'. This involved black students in segregated areas taking long bus rides to desegregated schools. Local white protests were organised to resist busing – such as the Restore Our Alienated Rights (ROAR) campaign in Boston during 1974. Nixon publicly supported the white protesters and refused to take any action to enforce the introduction of busing programmes. He also secured the appointment of three new conservative Supreme Court judges who, via the *Miliken v. Bradley* case of 1975, permitted the predominantly white Detroit suburbs to be excluded from a desegregation plan. President Gerald Ford, who succeeded Nixon after the latter's resignation from office in the wake of the Watergate scandal, pursued the same policy of non-intervention.

During the Nixon and Ford years, the only positive development for civil rights was the introduction of 'affirmative action' or positive discrimination employment programmes. As a result of the Philadelphia Plan of 1969, the Nixon administration required companies with Federal government contracts to increase their proportion of workers from ethnic minority groups to 26 per cent within four years. In *Giggs v. Duke Power Company* during 1971, the Supreme Court upheld the constitutionality of affirmative action. This resulted in over 300,000 businesses being bound by the new quotas by 1972.

The principle of 'affirmative action' was challenged in 1978 by white male student Alan Bakke, who claimed he was a victim of reverse discrimination because a minority student with lower test scores was admitted to the medical school in the University of California in his stead. Bakke appealed to the California Supreme Court, which upheld 'affirmative action', but ruled that the school's admission programme was unconstitutional and ordered the university to admit him.

Meanwhile, the gap continued to widen between the newly created African-American workforce and the great mass of unemployed blacks. Hence, Federal spending on welfare payments and social security doubled between January 1969 and August 1974. In 1975 Federal expenditure on food stamps amounted to $5,000 million, compared with only $36 million a year during the mid 1960s. Many racial problems continued to be unresolved, and even worsened towards the end of the 1980s. Yet some advances were undeniable. Owing to the efforts of the Congressional Black Caucus (CBC), established by black congressmen of all persuasions in 1971, there were over 40 African-American congressmen by the mid 1990s. In political terms African Americans had achieved electoral success unknown since the days of Black Reconstruction in the 1860s and 1870s.

Document case study

Civil rights in the Cold War

7.1 Elizabeth Eckford, one of the 'Little Rock Nine', tries to go to school on 3 September 1957

I saw a large crowd of people standing across the street from the soldiers guarding Central. As I walked on, the crowd suddenly got very quiet. Superintendent Blossom had told us to enter by the front door. I looked at all the people and thought, 'Maybe I will be safer if I walk down the block to the front entrance behind the guards.'

At the corner I tried to pass through the long line of guards around the school so as to enter the grounds behind them. One of the guards pointed across the street. So I pointed in the same direction and asked whether he meant for me to cross the street and walk down. He nodded 'yes'. So, I walked across the street conscious of the crowd that stood there, but they moved away from me.

For a moment all I could hear was the shuffling of their feet. Then someone shouted, 'Here she comes, get ready!' I moved away from the crowd on the sidewalk and into the street. If the mob came at me, I could then cross back over so the guards could protect me.

The crowd moved in closer and then began to follow me, calling me names. I still wasn't afraid. Just a little bit nervous. Then my knees started to shake all of a sudden and I wondered whether I could make it to the center entrance a block away. It was the longest block I ever walked in my whole life.

Even so, I still wasn't too scared because all the time I kept thinking that the guards would protect me.

When I got right in front of the school, I went up to a guard again. But this time he just looked straight ahead and didn't move to let me pass him. I didn't know what to do. Then I looked and saw that the path leading to the front entrance was a little further ahead. So I walked until I was right in front of the path to the front door.

I stood looking at the school—it looked so big! Just then the guards let some white students go through.

The crowd was quiet. I guess they were waiting to see what was going to happen. When I was able to steady my knees, I walked up to the guard who had let the white students in. He too didn't move. When I tried to squeeze past him, he raised his bayonet and then the other guards closed in and they raised their bayonets.

They glared at me with a mean look and I was very frightened and didn't know what to do. I turned around and the crowd came toward me.

They moved closer and closer. Somebody started yelling, 'Lynch her! Lynch her!'

I tried to see a friendly face somewhere in the mob—someone who maybe would help. I looked into the face of an old woman and it seemed a kind face, but when I looked at her again, she spat on me.

They came closer, shouting, 'No nigger bitch is going to get in our school. Get out of here!'

Source: Daisy Bates, *The long shadow of Little Rock*, New York: David McKay, 1962, pp. 73–75

7.2 Robert Weaver explains how blacks were disadvantaged by urban land and property developers

The authors of the most effective racial covenants are the subdividers who on their own initiative or under pressure from sources of finance cover new developments with these restrictive agreements. This is true for many reasons. Subdividers are the first commercial developers of urban land. As such, they transform raw land into building sites, laying out streets, planning land use, and often specifying, through deed restrictions, the use to which sites shall be put . . . Since, however, all this takes place before the occupant or ultimate owner moves into an area, patterns for residential segregation, effected by deed restrictions, occur without the active participation of the eventual parties to the agreement. Thus, subdividers and developers establish minority exclusion and patterns for its perpetuation without having to go to the expense of persuading purchasers to participate in the arrangement. And since new subdivisions are often occupied by the more prosperous elements in the population, patterns established in them become attractive to others who hope to become prosperous. When and if the latter group succeed in achieving this manifestation of arriving in our society, they, too, have little choice; if they want the sort of house that signifies prosperity, it is usually covered by a racial covenant.

Source: Robert C. Weaver, *The negro ghetto*, New York: Harcourt, Brace & Co., 1948, pp. 253–54

7.3 President John F. Kennedy's television and radio address to the American nation on 11 June 1963, in which he calls for equal rights

. . . This Nation was founded by men of many nations and backgrounds. It was founded on the principle that all men are created equal, and that the rights of every man are diminished when the rights of one man are threatened.

Today we are committed to a worldwide struggle to promote and protect the rights of all who wish to be free. And when Americans are sent to Viet-Nam or West Berlin, we do not ask for whites only. It ought to be possible, therefore, for American students of any color to attend any public institution they select without having to be backed up by troops . . . In short, every American ought to have the right to be treated as he would wish to be treated, as one would wish his children to be treated . . .

This is not a sectional issue. Difficulties over segregation and discrimination exist in every city, in every State of the Union, producing in many cities a rising tide of discontent that threatens the public safety. Nor is this a partisan issue . . . We are confronted primarily with a moral issue. It is as old as the scriptures and is as clear as the American Constitution.

The heart of the question is whether all Americans are to be afforded equal rights and equal opportunities, whether we are going to treat our fellow Americans as we want to be treated. If an American, because his skin is dark, cannot eat lunch in a restaurant open to the public, if he cannot send his children to the best public school available, if he cannot vote for the public officials who will represent him, if, in short, he cannot enjoy the full and free life which all of us want, then who among us would be content to have the color of his skin changed and stand in his place? Who among us would then be content with the counsels of patience and delay?

Source: *Public papers of the presidents of the United States: John F. Kennedy, 1963*, Washington DC: US Government Printing Office, 1964, vol. 3, pp. 236–37

7.4 From the speech delivered by Martin Luther King Jr on the steps at the Lincoln Memorial in Washington DC, 28 August 1963

I have a dream that one day this nation will rise up and live out the true meaning of its creed: 'We hold these truths to be self-evident: that all men are created equal.' I have a dream that one day on the red hills of Georgia the sons of former slaves and the sons of former slaveowners will be able to sit down together at a table of brotherhood. I have a dream that one day even the state of Mississippi . . . sweltering with the heat of injustice and oppression, will be transformed into an oasis of freedom and justice. I have a dream that my four children will one day live in a nation where they will not be judged by the color of their skin but by the content of their character.

Source: Martin Luther King Jr papers, 1954–68, Boston University, Boston, Massachusetts

7.5 Malcolm X explains 'black nationalism' at a New York press conference on 12 March 1964

The political philosophy of black nationalism means: we must control the politics and the politicians of our community. They must no longer take orders from outside forces. We will organize, and sweep out of office all Negro politicians who are puppets for the outside forces . . .

. . . Whites can help us, but they can't join us. There can be no black–white unity until there is first black unity. There can be no workers' solidarity until there is first some racial solidarity. We cannot think of uniting with others, until after we have first united among ourselves . . .

Concerning nonviolence: it is criminal to teach a man not to defend himself when he is the constant victim of brutal attacks. It is legal and lawful to own a shotgun or a rifle. We believe in obeying the law.

In areas where our people are the constant victims of brutality, and the government seems unable or unwilling to protect them, we should form rifle clubs that can be used to defend our lives and our property in times of emergency . . . When our people are being bitten by dogs, they are within their rights to kill those dogs.

We should be peaceful, law-abiding—but the time has come for the American Negro to fight back in self-defence whenever and wherever he is being unjustly and unlawfully attacked.

If the government thinks I am wrong for saying this, then let the government start doing its job.

Source: William Loren Katz, *Eyewitness: the negro in American history*, New York: Pittman Publishing Corporation, 1967, pp. 536–37

7.6 Langston Hughes, black poet, playwright, and author, takes a satirical look at the Harlem riot of 1964

Opinion in Harlem is divided as to whether or not riots do any good. Some say *yes*, they achieve concrete results in community improvements. Others say *no*, they set the Negro race back 50 years. Those who disagree say, in effect, 'But Negroes are always being set back 50 years by something or another, so what difference does a riot make?'

Old-timers who remember former riots in Harlem say, 'White folks respect us more when they find out we mean business. When they only listen to our speeches or read our writing—if they ever do—they think we are just blowing off steam. But when rioters smash the plate glass windows of their stores, they know the steam has some force behind it. Then they say, "The Negroes are mad! What do they want?" And for a little while they will try to give you a little of what you want . . .

. . . Negroes have been asking for years that Georgia and Mississippi be made safe—and getting no results from federal or state governments. But now, after a weekend of rioting in Harlem, you see what the President says! The riots have already produced one good result.

Source: Langston Hughes, 'Harlem III', *New York Post*, 23 July 1964, p. 29

7.7 From a speech by President Lyndon Baines Johnson on 15 March 1965, in the wake of racist attacks during the Selma March

I speak tonight for the dignity of man and the destiny of democracy . . . There is no Negro problem . . . There is only an American problem. And we are met here tonight as Americans, not as Democrats or Republicans, we are met here as Americans to solve that problem . . .

Every device of which human ingenuity is capable has been used to deny this right [to vote]. The Negro citizen may go to register only to be told that the day is wrong, or the hour is late, or the official in charge is absent. And if he persists and if he manages to present himself to the registrar, he may be disqualified because he did not spell out his middle name or because he abbreviated a word on the application. And if he manages to fill out the application he is given a test. The registrar is the sole judge of whether he passes this test. He may be asked to recite the entire constitution, or explain the most complex provisions of state laws. And even a college degree cannot be used to prove that he can read and write.

For the fact is that the only way to pass these barriers is to show a white skin . . .

Wednesday I will send to Congress a law designed to eliminate illegal barriers to the right to vote . . .

But even if we pass this bill, the battle will not be over. What happened in Selma is part of a far larger movement which reaches into every section and state of America. It is the effort of American Negroes to secure for themselves the full blessings of American life.

Their cause must be our cause too. Because it is not just Negroes, but really it is all of us, who must overcome the crippling legacy of bigotry and injustice. And we shall overcome . . .

The real hero of this struggle is the American Negro. His actions and protests, his courage to risk safety and even to risk his life, have awakened the conscience of this nation. His demonstrations have been designed to stir reform. He has called upon us to make good the promise of America. And who among us can say that we would have made the same progress were it not for his persistent bravery, and his faith in American democracy.

Source: Lyndon B. Johnson, Remarks of the president to a joint session of Congress (Washington DC: Office of the White House Press Secretary, 15 March 1965), pp. 1–5

Document case-study questions

1 What does Document 7.1 tell us about the difficulties black students faced during the early stages of integration?

2 What insights does Document 7.2 give into the development of black ghettos in American cities?

3 How does President John F. Kennedy's speech in Document 7.3 compare with his actions on civil rights up to that time?

4 Why may Martin Luther King's 'I have a dream' speech in Document 7.4 be described as the turning point in the struggle for civil rights?

5 Using Document 7.5 and the information in this chapter, what impact do you consider the disunity of African Americans had on their struggle for civil rights?

6 In what ways is the author of Document 7.6 critical of the civil rights movement?

7 In what way does President Lyndon Baines Johnson's speech in Document 7.7 compare with his actions on civil rights up to 1969?

Notes and references

1 Mary L. Dudziak, *Cold War civil rights*, Princeton, New Jersey, 2000, p. 3.

2 President's Committee on Civil Rights, *To secure these rights*, Washington DC: US Government Printing Office, 1947, p. 148.

3 *Supreme Court Reporter*, vol. 74, p. 693.

4 *Congressional Record, 84th Congress, 2nd Session*, vol. 102, part 4 (12 March 1956), Washington DC: US Government Printing Office, 1956, pp. 4459–60.

5 John F. Kennedy, 'Radio and television report to the American people on civil rights', 11 June 1963, *Public papers of the presidents of the United States: John F. Kennedy, 1963*, Washington DC: US Government Printing Office, 1964, vol. 3, p. 236.

6 Martin Luther King Jr papers, 1954–68, Boston University, Boston, Massachusetts.

7 Lyndon Baines Johnson, 'The president's news conference of March 13, 1965', *Public papers of the presidents of the United States: Lyndon Baines Johnson, 1965*, Washington DC: US Government Printing Office, 1966, vol. 1, p. 275.

8 Other minority rights

Growth of the US nation

Many other minority groups struggled for civil rights as the US nation expanded during the nineteenth and twentieth centuries. About 2.5 million people migrated to the United States during the 1850s. From 1860 to 1900 a further 14 million made the Atlantic crossing, while the first 40 years of the twentieth century saw over 18 million additional people arrive in America. Of these 35 million immigrants, the largest number was from the United Kingdom – some 16 million in total – of whom approximately 1.5 million came from Ireland. Germany accounted for about 4.5 million, and Scandinavia for about 2.75 million. The greater proportion of immigrants from northern and western Europe arrived in the New World during the decades immediately following the Civil War. A decline in immigration from the UK and Germany occurred after 1890 and from Scandinavia by the turn of the century.

'New immigration'

During the 1870s new types began to appear among the thousands of immigrants who swarmed in to Ellis Island, New York. These included Italians, Russians, Austrians, Poles, and Jews, plus other peoples from southern and eastern Europe. Known as the 'new immigration', this influx resulted from the economic and social changes that had earlier affected northern and western Europe – massive population increase, religious persecution, collapse of the old agricultural order, and industrial revolution.

Although many of these immigrants did settle in rural America, a great majority of them concentrated in the cities, particularly New York, Boston, Pittsburgh, and Chicago. Five out of every six Irish and Russian immigrants, and three out of four Italian and Hungarian immigrants, became city dwellers. Various reasons existed for this pattern of settlement. Many immigrants came to the United States with very little money to buy farms or expensive farming equipment. Others settled in cities because farming techniques in the New World were far different from what they had grown accustomed to in Europe. Some immigrants, such as the Slavs, simply arrived too late to acquire free or cheap land. Jewish immigrants preferred the cities because they provided a chance to worship with other Jews without fear of persecution. Many Irish settled in cities because working the land gave them painful memories of home, where English landlords had kept Irish tenant farmers in a constant state of oppression.

Physical examination of male immigrants on Ellis Island immigrant station during the 1920s.

Most immigrants, particularly the Irish and Italians, moved far more slowly into the next higher occupational stratum than the sons of middle- and upper-class Americans of Protestant English origin – who began with greater educational advantages and family financial backing. Irish Catholics were different in religion from the majority of Americans, but they spoke the same language. Many of the Germans and Scandinavians belonged to the Protestant majority and hence were able to make their way effectively, despite language barriers.

Opposition to the growing number of immigrants developed throughout the nineteenth century among the older 'native' Americans of white Protestant background. Before the Civil War, the American Party, or 'Know-Nothings', had developed from a number of nativist secret societies during the 1840s. Fearing a papal plot to subvert American values, its members initially convened in secret and developed numerous clandestine signals and signs. The Know-Nothings became a spent political force by 1854, largely owing to a temporary decline in immigration and disagreements within the party regarding policy. The American Protective League, founded in 1887 by Henry F. Bowers, was one of the largest and most powerful anti-immigrant and anti-Catholic organisations of the late nineteenth century. Claiming more than a million members by 1896, it was another nativist response to the large numbers of immigrants from Catholic countries. It spread anti-Catholic literature and propaganda. The revived Ku Klux Klan also extended its hatred towards Catholics and immigrants, as well as blacks, during the second decade of the twentieth century.

The 'science' of eugenics

Some of those wishing to limit the number of immigrants entering the United States invented the 'science' of eugenics to support their argument. Foreshadowing the later horrors of Nazi Germany, they claimed that cultural and social patterns were a result of heredity, and hence controllable through selective breeding. Leading eugenicists, such as Dr Charles Benedict Davenport, a biologist with a PhD from Harvard University, seized upon eugenics as a means of rationalising their racism 'scientifically'. In his book *Heredity in relation to eugenics* (1911), Davenport argued that weaknesses in society were due to the unnatural preservation of the 'feeble-minded' and 'unfit' by the use of modern medicine. Writing at a time when Italians, Poles, Greeks, Russians, and Jews were the targets of anti-immigrant phobia, Davenport suggested 'the population of the United States will, on account of the great influx of blood from South-eastern Europe, rapidly become darker in pigmentation, smaller in stature, more mercurial, more attached to music and art, [and] more given to crimes of larceny, kidnapping, assault, murder, rape and sex-immorality'.[1]

Others advocated less extreme means to achieve the same ends. As early as 1894 a group of prominent Boston lawyers, professors, and philanthropists formed the Immigration Restriction League to promote a literary test as a means of stemming the flow of immigrants. This action was condoned by the American Federation of Labor, which feared competition for jobs from immigrants. In 1907 the Immigration Commission (also known as the 'Dillingham Commission'), under its executive secretary William Walter Husband, was appointed by the US Senate to study immigration patterns. In its reports published in 1910–11, this body concluded that since the 1880s immigrants had been mainly of southern and eastern European stock. Influenced by the eugenics lobby, the commission assumed that immigrants from places like Austria–Hungary, Russia, Italy, Turkey, Lithuania, Romania, and Greece were inferior to the immigrants who had come before 1880, who were assumed to be of mainly northern and western European descent. The commission's 42-volume report recommended that literacy tests be used to deny inferior immigrants entry to the country.

Chinese citizenship

Different patterns of immigration emerged on the west coast of the United States during the nineteenth century, creating a large Chinese minority group. An unprecedented economic boom began in California following the discovery of gold in 1849. During the following two decades, thousands of workers, most of whom were male, were recruited from China by American employers to work in mining, railroad construction, and related service industries. The new immigrants were initially welcomed to California's gold fields and pioneer settlements. Even when the gold rush ended, there was plenty of work for Chinese labourers, although they were exploited by unscrupulous contractors who paid them only a minimal wage.

An agreement between the US and Chinese governments, known as the Burlingame Treaty – after the American minister to China, Anson Burlingame, was signed in Washington DC in July 1868. This amended the Treaty of Tientsin of 1858, which had permitted foreign economic exploitation of China. Under the terms of the Burlingame Treaty, both the United States and China were to recognise 'the inherent and inalienable right of man to change his home and allegiance, and also the mutual advantage of the free migration and emigration of their citizens and subjects, respectively for purposes of curiosity, of trade, or as permanent residents'. Another clause stipulated 'Chinese subjects visiting or residing in the United States, shall enjoy the same privileges, immunities, and exemptions in respect to travel or residence, as may there be enjoyed by the citizens or subjects of the most favored nation'. The privileges and immunities provision was aimed at protecting Chinese in the United States against discrimination, exploitation, and violence.

Following the passage of the Burlingame Treaty, an economic recession in the 1870s fostered a racist, anti-Chinese political movement in California. Led by Irish agitator Dennis Kearney, and taken up by the California Workingmen's Party and the Knights of Labor, 'nativists' blamed the Chinese for the current unemployment, and violent vigilante groups attacked Chinese communities and individuals throughout the region. In response, the California legislature attempted to bar the entry and settlement of Chinese nationals in the state via the Naturalization Act, but – under an 1849 Supreme Court decision reserving the power to control immigration to the Federal government – the Federal courts in California invalidated the state statutes. The anti-immigrant Californians remained undeterred, and went on to forge an alliance with east-coast nativists who shared their belief in the inherent intellectual and moral superiority of northern European Protestants. Preying on fears of labour militancy among immigrant workers, this faction gained support from big business for the first Federal laws restricting immigration.

In 1879 Congress failed in its attempt to pass the Fifteen Passenger Bill, designed to limit to 15 the number of Chinese passengers on board any ship landing in an American port. This bill was vetoed by President Rutherford B. Hayes, who argued that, by breaching the free immigration clause of the Burlingame Treaty, the bill was effectively a legislative nullification of a treaty with a friendly nation. He did not object to the goal of limiting Chinese immigration, only the means that Congress had chosen. In the process, he raised the possibility of revising the Burlingame Treaty.

In early 1880 Hayes appointed James Angell, former president of the University of Michigan, as chief negotiator for revising the Burlingame Treaty. In November the Burlingame Treaty Revision was signed, allowing the US government to suspend, but not prohibit, the immigration of Chinese labourers to the United States.

In March 1882 Congress passed the first Chinese Exclusion Bill, designed to ban the immigration of Chinese labourers to the United States for a period of 20 years. It also required Chinese already in residence in the country to carry an internal passport. Although permitted to travel freely throughout the United States, they were excluded from American citizenship. However, President

Chester Arthur vetoed the bill, believing that some of its restrictions were undemocratic. Congress was unable to override the presidential veto, and flags were hung at half-mast by nativists in San Francisco.

Supporters of the Exclusion Bill then reduced the period of suspension to ten years and dropped the passport provision. Chinese in the United States were still banned from becoming citizens but were allowed to travel freely, in accord with the 1880 revision of the Burlingame Treaty. President Arthur signed this bill into law on 6 May 1882. The Chinese Exclusion Act broke with the American tradition of open immigration and was the first Federal law aimed at restricting a specifically named ethnic group.

Three months later Congress passed a general immigration law that levied a one-off 50-cent tax on all new immigrants and also excluded persons in certain categories – such as convicted criminals, the insane, and those likely to become taxpayer supported – from entering American territory. The prohibition on Chinese immigration was extended in 1890 and again in 1902 until it became permanent. As a result of this policy of exclusion, the Chinese population in the United States declined from 107,000 to 75,000 by 1930.

The 'Gentleman's Agreement'

Growing Japanese influence in Asia at the beginning of the twentieth century was accompanied by the settlement of increased numbers of Japanese immigrants along the west coast of America. Known as *Issei*, these first-generation Japanese immigrants were denied the opportunity to become naturalised as citizens. A treaty between the United States and Japan in 1894 had assured free immigration, but as the number of Japanese workers in California increased, they were met with growing hostility. In August 1900 Japan agreed to deny passports to labourers seeking to enter the United States. This did not stop the many workers who obtained passports to Canada, Mexico, or Hawaii from moving on to the United States. Fed by inflammatory 'Yellow Peril' articles in the press, racial antagonism continued to intensify until, on 7 May 1906, the San Francisco School Board arranged for all Asian children in the city to be placed in a segregated school.

Japan was prepared to limit immigration to the United States, but was deeply offended by the discriminatory San Francisco law aimed specifically at its people. Wishing to preserve good relations with Japan as a counter to Russian expansion in the Far East, President Theodore Roosevelt intervened. While the American ambassador reassured the Japanese government, Roosevelt summoned the San Francisco mayor and school board to the White House in February 1907 and persuaded them to rescind the segregation order, promising that the Federal government would address the question of immigration. On 4 February the 'Gentleman's Agreement' with Japan was concluded in the form of a Japanese note agreeing to deny passports to labourers intending to enter the United States, and recognising the US right to exclude Japanese immigrants holding passports originally issued for other countries. This was followed by the formal withdrawal of the San Francisco School Board order on 13 March 1907. A final Japanese note dated 18 February 1908 made the Gentleman's Agreement fully effective. The agreement was superseded by the exclusionary Immigration Act of 1924, which completely barred all immigration from China and Japan.

On the eve of the Japanese attack on Pearl Harbor on 7 December 1941, there were 127,000 Japanese Americans, of whom 62.7 per cent were citizens by birth. In addition, 158,000 people of Japanese origin lived in the Territory of Hawaii and 263 in the Territory of Alaska. Following the 'day of infamy', a total of 112,000 people of Japanese ancestry, 71,000 of whom were American citizens or *Nisei*, were removed from their homes along the Pacific coast and placed in internment camps in the interior. These people had personal possessions such as radios, cameras, and binoculars confiscated, and spent the rest of the war behind barbed wire, guarded by the US Army. However, only five thousand renounced their American citizenship, while the great majority remained loyal to the United States. Strangely, only a small number of the Japanese residents on Hawaii were similarly interned.

Immigration since 1945

With the advent of the Cold War, advocates for immigration reform argued that if the United States wished to portray itself as a leader of the 'free world' it would have to eliminate racial discrimination – not only in all domestic aspects of public life, but also in immigration policy. Opponents of the National Origins Act of 1929 were unsuccessful in their efforts to introduce full-scale reform. As a result of this Act, the annual immigrant quota had been reduced to 150,000 Europeans, to be apportioned among the various countries in proportion to the 'national origins' of the American people in 1920. Although the McCarran Walter Act of 1952 permitted a token number of non-European immigrants per year (2,990 Asians and 1,400 Africans, compared with 149,667 from Europe), it also strengthened the attorney general's authority to exclude or deport aliens suspected of supporting communism.

President Harry Truman authorised a commission to investigate the social and political implications of US immigration policy in 1953. However, it required the civil rights movement, and the election of John F. Kennedy as the first Catholic president, to create a climate in which Congress would finally lift the 'national origins' quota.

As a result of the Immigration and Naturalization Act of 1965, which was not fully implemented until June 1968, the 'national origins' quotas were abolished. These were replaced by the present system of granting lawful permanent residence based on job skills or close family relationships with US citizens or lawful permanent residents. The new 'preference' system established a labour certification programme, and imposed a ceiling on western hemisphere immigration. The eastern hemisphere was allocated a total of 170,000 visas per year, with a maximum of 20,000 per country; while the western hemisphere got 120,000 a year, without any country ceilings. In addition, the spouse, unmarried children, and parents of US citizens were permitted to enter as non-quota immigrants without numerical limit. The latter ruling had unexpected consequences. Floods of Asian immigrants took the opportunity of joining relatives in the United States. Asians, including Vietnamese and Chinese, composed more than half of the total influx.

However, certain minority groups from other parts of the world continued to experience difficulties. Hispanic people involved in the exodus from the Batista regime, or from the subsequent Castro revolution, in Cuba were generally relocated and educated in southern Florida and became a part of US society. Between 1959 and 1962, 274,000 Cubans 'emigrated' to the United States. The Cuban Adjustment Act passed on 2 November 1966 allowed Cuban migrants who reached US shores after 1 January 1959 to remain. While almost 50 per cent of those who arrived were professionals, proprietors, technicians, and managers, they faced great difficulty in competing against 'older Americans' in the labour market. By 1966 only 13 per cent of those who reached US shores after 1959 held their original professions and jobs, while 32 per cent of them were unskilled labourers, double the proportion among those entering the country.

Chicanos

It was the exclusion of Chinese in the 1880s that forced US employers to turn to Mexico to recruit a labour force. The invention of large-scale irrigation technology and railroad development had opened up access to potential east-coast markets for fruits and vegetables. All that was lacking in the thinly populated state of California and the south-west was the labour to produce the crops. Meanwhile, the deterioration of economic conditions in Mexico, plus a revolution that lasted from 1910 to 1920, led to a steady flow of low-skilled labour north of the border. It continued throughout the pre-First World War period. With the conscription of a million young Americans into the US armed forces from 1917 to 1918, opportunities opened up in industry as well.

Approximately 1.5 million Mexicans were domiciled in the United States by 1930, the vast majority of them in the border states of Texas, New Mexico, Arizona, and California. Mexican communities also grew in the industrial mid-west cities of Chicago, Milwaukee, and Detroit. The Depression brought Mexican immigration to a temporary halt and, in fact, reversed the flow as thousands of Mexicans, thrown out of work along with their US co-workers, were denied local charitable aid and sought Mexican government help to return home.

The US entry into the Second World War, with the accompanying acceleration of industrial and agricultural production and a further draft of over one million American men, forced the US government to turn once again to Mexico to fill essential jobs. By treaty, the US and Mexican governments agreed to facilitate and monitor the recruitment of Mexican workers by US employers. The resulting *Bracero* programme, as it came to be called, brought thousands of Mexican workers through official channels to America's factories, farms, and transportation facilities. This programme was renewed by treaty several times. From 1941 until 1964, 4.6 million *braceros* worked in the United States for short periods, earning wages lower than those received by domestic workers. In 1965 a new

US–Mexican agreement permitted growers to recommence the importation of Mexican workers, provided they were paid no more than $1.25 an hour.

The plight of the *Chicanos*, as Mexican Americans prefer to be called, became a focus of the civil rights movement during the post-war years. In 1954 *Hernandez v. Texas* became the first Mexican-American discrimination case to reach the Supreme Court. The case involved the murder conviction of Pete Hernandez by a jury that did not contain a single jurist of Hispanic origin. Chief Justice Earl Warren held that people of Mexican descent were 'persons of a distinct class' entitled to the protection of the 14th Amendment.

On the political front, José Angel Gutiérrez founded the Mexican American Youth Organization in San Antonio, Texas, during 1967. This group developed into La Rasa Unida Party, the first *Chicano* political party. During the same year, articles of incorporation were filed in San Antonio for the Mexican American Legal Defense and Education Fund (MALDEF), the first national *Chicano* civil rights legal organisation. Furthermore, a campaign for educational reform made steady progress in school desegregation, the development of bilingual and bicultural courses, and the recruitment of more *Chicano* teachers and administrators.

Meanwhile, Arizona-born Cesar E. Chávez became the leading spokesperson for *Chicano* civil and trade-union rights. In collaboration with Dolores Huerta, he founded the National Farm Workers Association (NFWA) in 1962. By 1965 the NFWA had recruited farm workers throughout the San Joaquin Valley of California. On 8 September of that year Filipino members of the Agricultural Workers Organizing Committee (AWOC), led by Larry Dulay Itliong, demanded higher wages and called the grape-growing labourers in the Delano area out on strike. Although the NFWA had planned to organise farm workers for several more years before confronting the large corporate grape industry, they could not ignore the actions of the AWOC, and joined the strike. Over five thousand grape workers walked off their jobs and took part in an action that would last five years. The two organisations merged in 1966 to form the United Farm Workers Organizing Committee (UFWOC), eventually known as the United Farm Workers of America (UFWA).

In order to obtain better pay and conditions, and the right to join a union, Cesar Chávez continued to campaign, using non-violent tactics such as boycotts and pickets against the fruit and vegetable growers of California and the south-west. Millions of American consumers, already focused on the civil rights movement associated with African Americans, acknowledged the plight of the *Chicano* and Filipino farm labourers and stopped buying table grapes. In March 1966 Chávez led a protest march from Delano to Sacramento, the state capital of California, to draw national attention to the problems facing the farm workers. It started with only 75 supporters, but 10,000 people were present at the rally when the demonstration finally reached its destination about a month later. Among the many other civil rights groups joining the UFWOC strike efforts were the black SNCC and CORE.

By the late 1960s UFWA had gained national recognition, and the California farm workers had become part of 'The Movement' – a catch-all term describing

Cesar Chávez, co-founder of the NFWA, talking to striking grape-pickers in California in 1970.

those groups sharing a commitment to end the injustices of racism, the war in Vietnam, and the sufferings of the poor. At the forefront of the battle was Cesar Chávez, who fasted, marched, and boycotted in support of social change and civil rights until his death in 1993.

Native Americans

Since 1900 the Native American population of America has increased to about one million people, who mainly live west of the Mississippi in the states of Oklahoma, Arizona, and California. Although predominantly from a rural culture, large numbers of them were encouraged by government-sponsored relocation programmes to move into cities, as a means of relieving chronic unemployment, illiteracy, alcoholism, and the high mortality rates of the reservations. It was also hoped that they would be integrated into white society. By 1980 almost 50 per cent of Native Americans were urban dwellers, many of them living in small towns close to reservations. Others congregated in larger metropolitan areas such as San Francisco, Los Angeles, and Tulsa. Most became overwhelmed by the impersonality of city life, and found great difficulty in escaping exploitation, poverty, and discrimination. However, the urban experience also stimulated a feeling of pan-Indian identity. Freed from the conservative restraints of tribal council communities, the younger generation of Indian leaders began to protest against their unequal status in American society.

The American Indian Movement (AIM) was established by Ojibwa activists George Mitchell, Dennis Banks, and Clyde Bellecourt in Minneapolis during 1968. Influenced by the black civil rights movement, this group used direct action to demonstrate against the plight of the Native American people. On 9 November 1969, 78 Indians – led by Richard Oakes, a Mohawk who directed Indian studies at San Francisco State College, and Grace Thorpe, a Sac and Fox Indian who was the daughter of Jim Thorpe, the famous Indian college football star and Olympic athlete – occupied Alcatraz Island in San Francisco Bay. Others joined them and by the end of November nearly six hundred Native Americans, representing more than fifty tribes, were living on Alcatraz. They called themselves the 'Indians of all Tribes' and issued a proclamation entitled 'We hold the rock'. In it they offered to buy Alcatraz with glass beads and red cloth, the form of payment made to Indians for Manhattan Island over three hundred years earlier. They also announced they would make the island a centre for Native American studies for ecology, claiming: 'We will work to de-pollute the air and waters of the Bay Area . . . restore fish and animal life.' In the months that followed, the government cut off electricity, water, and telephones to Alcatraz Island. Many of the demonstrators had to leave, but others insisted on staying. Nineteen months later Federal forces invaded the island and removed those who remained.

To comply with Indian grievances, the Nixon administration appointed a Mohawk-Sioux called Louis R. Bruce as commissioner for Indian affairs and returned 48,000 acres (19,000 hectares) of sacred tribal lands to the Taos-Pueblo people.

In 1972 an AIM-backed march on Washington, known as the Trail of Broken Treaties, culminated in the occupation of the Bureau of Indian Affairs (BIA) headquarters. The demonstrators presented a 20-point 'position paper' to President Richard Nixon. It included a demand for the restoration of constitutional treaty-making authority, and the establishment of a commission to review treaty commitments and violations. Similar protests followed, such as the Trail of Self-determination in 1976 and the Longest Walk in 1978. On the latter occasion, members of the 'Indian nations' walked across the United States from California to Washington DC to protest against anti-Indian legislation calling for the abrogation of treaties.

In 1973 about three hundred Oglala-Sioux, many of whom were members of AIM, occupied the village of Wounded Knee, the site of the massacre by the US Army of three hundred Indians in 1890. Declaring it liberated territory, they vowed to stay until the government agreed to address Native American grievances. A 72-day siege by Federal marshals ended when the Indians surrendered in exchange for a promise of negotiations. The Federal government did little immediately, however, to help their plight.

In 1975 the Nixon administration passed the Indian Self-determination and Education Assistance Act, which gave Native Americans the right to choose their own form of government, although being ultimately answerable to the BIA. The Indian Health Care Improvement Act of 1976, the Indian Child Welfare Act of 1978, and the Indian Religious Act of 1978 also brought some relief and support.

Meanwhile, other Native Americans took a less militant course of action. In 1970 the California Indian Legal Service (CILS) was established. Funded by the Ford Foundation, and mainly staffed and run by Indians, this organisation was created to assist in alleviating legal issues facing the Native American people. One year later CILS relocated to Boulder, Colorado, where it became known as the Native American Rights Fund (NARF) and set about helping Indians on a national level. Within a few years NARF grew from a 3-lawyer staff to a firm of 40 full-time staff members, plus 15 attorneys. By 1994 over 19,000 NARF clients had received legal representation. Since 1986 organisations such as Night Walker have also worked to relieve distress on the reservations of Native Americans by fund-raising and distributing food and clothing.

Women's rights

Although not a minority numerically, women have historically been relegated to a secondary position in US society. The earliest efforts to gain equality for women occurred in the 1840s, and were pioneered by the Grimké sisters, Lucy Stone, and Philadelphia Quaker Lucretia Mott. 'Men and women are created equal,' wrote Sarah Grimké. 'They are both moral and accountable beings, and whatever is right for man to do, is *right* for woman.'[2] These efforts were initially interwoven with the abolitionist movement, but discrimination impelled its champions to make women's rights a separate cause. In 1848 Lucretia Mott and Elizabeth Cady Stanton organised a women's rights convention at Seneca Falls, New York, and proclaimed their Declaration of Sentiment, which was based on the Declaration of Independence. Twelve resolutions were passed on this occasion, although the call for women's suffrage failed to gain unanimous support.

None the less, the movement to enfranchise women gathered momentum following the Civil War when feminists attempted to gain woman suffrage as part of the 14th Amendment to the Constitution. When this failed, the National Association for Woman Suffrage was established in 1868, with Stanton and Susan B. Anthony as its leaders. Meanwhile, a rival organisation called the American Woman Suffrage Association, led by Julia Ward Howe and Lucy Stone, appeared. These two groups coalesced in 1890 to form the National American Woman Suffrage Association (NAWSA).

Progress towards female suffrage was slow because of male prejudice and an unwillingness to allow women to become involved in the 'sordid business of politics'. Thus by 1900 only the western states of Colorado, Idaho, Utah, and Wyoming had granted full voting rights to women. However, NAWSA membership soared from 17,000 to 2 million between 1905 and 1917. The American suffragists did not adopt the militant tactics of their British counterparts, who were involved in slashing paintings, destroying post-boxes, and disrupting public meetings and sporting events. In fact, Carrie Chapman Catt and Dr Anna Howard Shaw, the dominant NAWSA leaders, furiously denounced any form of militancy, and in 1913 a women's suffrage march on Washington DC was easily broken up by a mob.

Susan B. Anthony and Elizabeth Cady Stanton, leaders of the movement for women's rights in the nineteenth century.

As in Britain, the First World War undermined opposition to women's suffrage. Women came out of the home and replaced men in the factories and offices, and on the land. Their contribution to the war effort made their demand for suffrage and political equality difficult to resist. Under Carrie Chapman Catt's shrewd direction, NAWSA adopted the so-called Winning Plan with widespread grassroots support. In 1917 New York became the first east-coast state to enfranchise women, and during January 1918 the House of Representatives adopted the 19th Amendment to the Constitution, providing for female suffrage. Although this measure was blocked in the Senate by Southerners for more than a year, it was finally ratified in June 1919 and went into effect in August 1920.

The 'women's liberation movement'

Once suffrage had been achieved, the campaign to further women's rights fell on hard times, remaining without focus until the 1950s, when it became associated with the 'rights revolution'. Concern about the image of the United States abroad during the Cold War sparked off a series of campaigns at home that promoted social justice and personal rights, including 'feminism'. Official awareness of feminism was heightened in 1963 when the Presidential Commission on the Status of Women, established by President John F. Kennedy, published its report on sexual discrimination in employment. This documented occupational inequities experienced by women that were similar to those suffered by minority groups. Women were paid less than men for doing the same work, and had far less opportunity to gain promotion or develop managerial careers. While women composed 51 per cent of the population, only 7 per cent of the nation's doctors and 4 per cent of its lawyers were female.[3]

Title VII of the Civil Rights Act of 1964 established the Equal Employment Opportunity Commission (EEOC), which prohibited employment discrimination on 'the basis of race, color, religion, sex, or national origin'. Coming into operation on 2 July 1965, this agency appeared to display a reluctance to enforce the ban on discrimination by gender. Hence in 1966 Betty Friedan, Bella Abzug, and others formed the National Organization for Women (NOW), a feminist civil rights group which lobbied for equal opportunity and filed law-suits against gender discrimination.

Support for NOW was to some extent based on Betty Friedan's *The feminine mystique* (1963), which condemned the narrow post-war view that women should find fulfilment solely as wives and mothers. Feminism found another catalyst with the involvement of younger women in the civil rights and anti-Vietnam War movements. By 1967 female veterans of these groups launched a new campaign for women's liberation that borrowed the concept of class oppression from Marxist political theory, and combined this with the rhetoric and actions of the African-American movement for equality. During 1968 female activists employed a variety of tactics as a means of recruitment. Tens of thousands of women met in small 'consciousness-raising' discussion groups to share experiences and air grievances. They also crowned a live sheep as 'Miss America', and produced 'freedom trash cans' in which women could discard bras, hair curlers, and high-heeled shoes. Furthermore, they invaded all-male bars and clubs, and sat in on meetings of lawyers' associations and medical societies to highlight discrimination against women in the professions. To commemorate the fiftieth anniversary of women's suffrage, the Women's Strike for Equality was organised on 26 August 1970, resulting in 50,000 women marching down Fifth Avenue in New York to demand the right to equal opportunity and employment.

In 1971 Bella Abzug, Betty Friedan, and Representative Shirley Chisholm formed the National Women's Political Caucus to make women more visible in politics. Within 12 months not only had there been significant increases in the number of women at national party conventions, but Shirley Chisholm had become the first black woman to campaign for presidential nomination.

Equal Rights Amendment

The campaign to amend the Constitution in order to secure equal rights for women began in 1921 when Alice Paul, leader of the National Woman's Party, wrote the Equal Rights Amendment (ERA). This was based on the premise that, despite the passage of the 14th Amendment, 'equal justice under law' had yet to be fully extended to women. ERA was introduced into every session of Congress between 1923 and 1972, when it was finally passed but ratified by only 28 states, 10 short of the number required for full ratification. The 7-year time limit in the proposing clause for ERA was extended by Congress to 30 June 1982, but at the deadline it had been ratified by only 35 states, leaving it 3 short of the required number. It has been reintroduced into every Congress since that time, but has yet to become the 28th Amendment to the Constitution.

The 'rights revolution'

Under the influence of Chief Justice Earl Warren, and in response to Cold War pressures, the Supreme Court was responsible during the period 1953 to 1969 for a series of decisions that promoted a number of social justice and personal rights issues throughout the United States. Between 1950 and 1954 Senator Joseph McCarthy had conducted an anti-communist witch-hunt that needlessly blackened reputations and ruined the lives of innocent people. On 17 June 1957 the Supreme Court held in the case of *Yates v. United States* that mere membership of the Communist Party was not sufficient evidence for a conviction on a charge of conspiracy to overthrow the government by force. Regarding religious instruction in public education, the court declared via the cases of *Engel v. Vitale* (1962) and *Abington Township v. Schempp* (1963) that prayers and Bible-reading in public schools were violations of the constitutional principle of the separation of church from state. A new code of criminal procedure was created via a series of cases, beginning with *Gideon v. Wainwright* (1963) and culminating with *Miranda v. Arizona* (1966). As a result, suspects were provided with the right to remain silent and to consult a lawyer before being questioned. Of equal significance were the court's decisions in *Baker v. Carr* (1962) and *Reynolds v. Sims* (1964), which equalised electoral districts and thereby ended the rural dominance of state legislatures.

In 1973 Congress passed the Vocation Rehabilitation Act, Section 504 of which provided Federal funds to help eliminate discrimination against disabled people. The right of abortion, which is central to the current controversy between 'pro-life' and 'pro-choice' advocates, was granted to American women during the same year as a result of the landmark case of *Roe v. Wade*. Prior to this case, the legality of abortion essentially rested with the legislatures of the separate states, which maintained that there was no constitutional right to abortion. However, in 1973 the Supreme Court ruled that Jane Roe had been denied a medically safe abortion and that this abridged her personal privacy, guarded by the 14th Amendment to the Constitution. From then on, whether abortion was legal or not depended on the Supreme Court's decision regarding how broad the *Roe* right to abortion actually was.

Gay rights

The events in New York City on 27 June 1969 marked the beginning of the gay liberation movement. New York's tactical police force regularly raided a popular Greenwich Village gay bar called the Stonewall Inn, but that night the street erupted into violent protest as the crowd in the bar fought back. The backlash plus several nights of protest that followed have come to be known as the Stonewall Riots.

By 1973 the 'rights revolution' began to impact on the gay rights movement when the Board of Trustees of the American Psychiatric Association voted unanimously to strike from its manuals the classification of homosexuality as a mental illness. On 14 October 1979 the first gay and lesbian civil rights march on

Washington drew more than 100,000 people. In 1983 Gerry Studds, a Democratic representative for Massachusetts, became the first member of Congress to acknowledge his homosexuality publicly. During the same year, the American Federation of Labor and the Congress of Industrial Organizations (AFL-CIO) voted to support gay rights legislation at Federal, state, and local levels. This was the first labour organisation to take such a stand. Between 250,000 and 500,000 gay men, lesbians, and their supporters again converged on Washington DC in 1985, for the largest gay rights demonstration ever held in the United States. By 1993 eight states had passed gay rights legislation. The civil rights of lesbians and gay men were recognised by the Supreme Court for the first time in 1996 in *Romer v. Evans*, when a Colorado state constitutional amendment passed by public referendum, which prohibited the state and its municipalities from enacting gay rights laws, was invalidated.

A conservative backlash to the 'rights revolution' occurred during the presidencies of Ronald Reagan and George Bush, from 1980 to 1992, resulting in the appointment of judges – including the resolutely conservative Chief Justice William H. Rehnquist – who undid aspects of 'rights revolution' legislation. For example, in 1984 the Supreme Court ruled that states did have the right to outlaw homosexual acts between consenting adults. In the cases of *Webster v. Reproductive Health Services* in 1989 and *Planned Parenthood v. Casey* in 1992, the Supreme Court re-examined the authority the states had over abortion, and allowed those that wished to regulate abortion substantially more latitude to do so.

Document case study

Other minority rights

8.1 Extract from an article by Francis A. Walker, a leading proponent of immigration restriction in the late nineteenth century

It is true that in the past there has been gross and scandalous neglect of this matter [of immigration] on the part both of government and people, here in the United States. For nearly two generations, great numbers of persons utterly unable to earn their living, by reason of one or another form of physical or mental disability, and others who were, from widely different causes, unfit to be members of any decent community, were admitted to our ports without challenge or question. It is a matter of official record that in many cases these persons had been directly shipped to us by states or municipalities desiring to rid themselves of a burden and a nuisance; while it could reasonably be believed that the proportion of such instances was far greater than could be officially ascertained. But all this is of the past. The question of the restriction of immigration to-day does not deal with that phase of the subject. What is proposed is, not to keep out some hundreds, or possibly thousands of persons, against whom lie specific objections like those above indicated, but to exclude perhaps hundreds of thousands, the great majority of whom would be subject to no individual objections; who, on the contrary, might fairly be expected to earn their living here in this new country, at least up to the standard known to them at home, and probably much more. The question to-day is, not of preventing the wards of our almshouses, our insane asylums, and our jails from being stuffed to repletion by new arrivals from Europe; but of protecting the American rate of wages, the American standard of living, and the quality of American citizenship from degradation through the tumultuous access of vast throngs of ignorant and brutalized peasantry from the countries of eastern and southern Europe.

Source: Francis A. Walker, 'Restriction of immigration', *The Atlantic Monthly* (June 1896), vol. 77, no. 464; pp. 822–23

8.2 Notice published by the Knights of Labor, a trade union movement, in response to the growing numbers of Chinese working in the laundry industry in the 1870s

TO THE PUBLIC:

MEN FROM CHINA come here to do LAUNDRY WORK. The Chinese Empire contains 600,000,000 inhabitants. The supply of these men is inexhaustible. Every one doing this work takes BREAD from the mouths of OUR WOMEN. So many have come of late, that to keep at work, they are obliged to cut prices. And now, we appeal to the public, asking them will they be partners to a deal which is only one of their many onward marches in CRUSHING OUT THE INDUSTRIES OF OUR COUNTRY from our people by grasping them themselves. Will you oblige the AMERICAN LAUNDRIES to CUT THE WAGES OF THEIR PEOPLE by giving your patronage to the CHINAMEN?

We invite you to give a thorough investigation of the STEAM LAUNDRY BUSINESS of the country; in doing so you will find that not only does it GIVE EMPLOYMENT TO A VAST NUMBER OF WOMEN, but a great field of labor is opened to a great number of mechanics of all kinds whose wages are poured back into the trade of the country. If this undesirable element 'THE CHINESE EMIGRANTS' are not stopped coming here . . . the end will be that our industries will be absorbed UNLESS we live down to their animal life.

We say in conclusion that the CHINAMAN is a labor consumer of our country without the adequate returns of prosperity to our land as is given by the labor of our people to our glorious country. Our motto should be: OUR COUNTRY, OUR PEOPLE, GOD, AND OUR NATIVE LAND.

Pioneer Laundry Workers Assembly, K. of L. Washington DC

Source: Thomas Magee, *Knights of Labor, 'China's menace to the world'*, Washington DC: Library of Congress, 1878

8.3 Report summarising anti-Chinese sentiment among the labour movement in the 1870s

. . . the true credit for the agitation against Oriental Immigration should go where it belongs – to the pioneers of the trade union movement in San Francisco, Dennis Kearney, Frank Rooney, John O. Walsh, John I. Nolan, and many others of that day who in and out of season preached the gospel of exclusion of Orientals.

Source: 'Proceedings of the Forty-third Annual Convention of the California State Federation of Labor, Long Beach, California', 21–25 September 1942, *New Politics*, vol. 8, no. 1 (new series), whole no. 29 (summer 2000)

8.4 Contemporary account of how the state of Texas treated migrant agricultural workers of Mexican origin

This is an average picture of what happened in 1944. On one Saturday afternoon in October of that year, 496 migratory labor trucks were counted on the streets of Lubbock, the 'capital' of the cotton-raising Plains area. Lubbock is a city of between 40,000 to 50,000 inhabitants. Each truck carried an average fifteen migrants, of all ages, which meant an estimated total of 7,440 migrants who had come to Lubbock to spend the weekend, seek new opportunities for employment, purchase their groceries and other supplies for the following week, and find a little recreation.

Large crews have been known to spend as much as $100.00 in one day, just in the purchase of groceries, during the peak of the season. But to make a very conservative estimate, let us suppose that each of the 496 crews in Lubbock that weekend spent an average of $25.00. That is a total of $12,400.00 income to business places of all kinds in one weekend.

Yet Lubbock has made no provision whatever for taking care of this influx of people, which occurs regularly every fall, and every weekend during each fall. There was no place where they might park their trucks, take a bath, change their clothes, even go to the toilet.

Conditions in towns throughout that section of the State were, in 1944, more or less the same as in Lubbock. In some places they were even worse. In Lamesa it was stated in the meeting that toilet facilities in the City Hall, which the migrants could use more conveniently, were locked up at noon on Saturdays, and filling station facilities were used except where the owners prohibited it because of the objections of customers. As a result, the migrants were forced to disregard the lack of toilet facilities, and an epidemic of dysentery, which originated among them, spread through the entire town of Lamesa and into the schools.

Source: Pauline R. Kibbe, *Latin Americans in Texas*, University of New Mexico Press, Albuquerque, 1946, pp. 177–78

8.5 Proclamation issued by the Native Americans who occupied Alcatraz Island on 9 November 1969

We feel that this so-called Alcatraz Island is more than suitable for an Indian reservation, as determined by the white man's own standards. By this we mean that this place resembles most Indian reservations in that:

1. It is isolated from modern facilities, and without adequate means of transportation.
2. It has no fresh running water.
3. It has inadequate sanitation facilities.
4. There are no oil or mineral rights.
5. There is no industry and so unemployment is very great.
6. There are no health care facilities.
7. The soil is rocky and non-productive; and the land does not support game.
8. There are no educational facilities.
9. The population has always exceeded the land base.
10. The population has always been held as prisoners and dependent upon others.

Source: The Indians of all nations, 'We hold the rock', Fourth World Documentation Project, Center for World Indigenous Studies

8.6 Speech by Senator Robert L. Owen of Oklahoma, who had earlier demanded citizenship for Native Americans, supporting women's suffrage in 1910

Women compose one-half of the human race. In the last forty years, women in gradually increasing numbers have been compelled to leave the home and enter the factory and workshop. Over seven million women are so employed, and the remainder of the sex are employed largely in domestic services. A full half of the work of the world is done by women. A careful study of the matter has demonstrated the vital fact that these working women receive a smaller wage for equal work than men do, and that the smaller wage and harder conditions imposed on the woman worker are due to the lack of the ballot.

Source: *Annals of the American Academy of Political and Social Science*, vol. 35, supplement (May 1910), p. 69

8.7 Mrs Gilbert E. Jones, an opponent of votes for women and a member of the Anti-Suffragist League, pleads her case

A very conscientious investigation by this League cannot find that the ballot will help the wage earning woman. Women must resort to organization, association, and trade unions, and then they can command and maintain a standard wage. Supply and demand will do the rest. Women are not well trained and often very deficient and unskilled in most of their occupations. They are generally only supplementary workers and drop their work when they marry. When married, and home and children are to be cared for, they are handicapped way beyond their strength. Married women should be kept out of industry, rather than urged into it, as scientists, physicians, and sociologists all state that as women enter into competitive industrial life with men, just so does the death rate of little children increase and the birth rate decrease.

Source: *Annals of the American Academy of Political and Social Science*, vol. 35, supplement (May 1910), p. 17

8.8 A leading figure in the women's liberation movement in America comments on women's rights

Women have every 'right' to be completely outraged when they become aware of the kind of outright and subtle oppression they suffer and that their sisters throughout the world suffer. They have every 'right' to be outraged at the indifference of men to their plight, their willingness to reap advantages until it is no longer possible. But just as might does not make right, nor does right make right. That is, one does not then have the right to play the same game with the tables turned. If one does this, one is playing society's game, for that is what this society is all about: absorption is its game.

Source: Roxanne Dunbar, 'Who is the enemy?', *No more Fun and Games: a Journal of Female Liberation*, cell 16, vol. 1, no. 2 (February 1969)

Document case-study questions

1 What objections to immigration are given in Document 8.1?

2 With what justification, according to Documents 8.2 and 8.3, was the labour movement anti-Chinese?

3 In what ways is Document 8.4 useful in assessing the difficulties faced by Mexican *braceros* in 1944?

4 What light does Document 8.5 shed on the plight of Native Americans by 1969?

5 Compare the views on women's suffrage offered in Documents 8.6 and 8.7. How are they similar or different?

6 Explain the philosophy towards women's rights presented in Document 8.7.

Notes and references

1 Charles Benedict Davenport, *Heredity in relation to eugenics*, New York: Arno Press/The New York Times, 1972. Facsimile of 1911 edition.

2 Paul S. Boyer *et al.*, *The enduring vision: a history of the American people*, Lexington, Massachusetts: D. C. Heath & Company, 1996, pp. 325–26.

3 Sheila Rowbotham, *A century of women: the history of women in Britain and the United States*, London: Penguin Books, 1997, p. 371.

Conclusion

The story of civil rights in America does not have a happy ending. While considerable progress has been made since the abolition of slavery in 1865, much remains to be achieved before the 'unalienable rights' of all American citizens are fully realised. Progress made during the protest days of the 1960s has given way in the 1980s, 1990s, and first decade of the twenty-first century to a further period of conservatism and accommodation.

The influence of organisations such as the NAACP, CORE, and the SNCC has nearly vanished. In the last two decades of the twentieth century the NAACP was troubled by financial and organisational problems, while CORE and the SNCC disappeared from public life. During the twentieth century's closing years, many of the leading figures of civil rights and black power faded into the pages of history. In 1989 the Black Panther leader Huey P. Newton was shot dead in Oakland. During 1998 black power icon Stokely Carmichael died of prostate cancer in Guinea, West Africa. In 1999 James Farmer, co-founder and former head of CORE, died aged 79 after several years of ill health. Others, such as Jesse Jackson and Louis Farrakhan, who became the leader of the Nation of Islam in 1977, emerged to take their place. Like their worthy predecessors, they fought to overcome the problems that continue to beset African Americans and other minority groups in the United States.

In 1895 Booker T. Washington used his Atlanta Compromise speech to advise his fellow blacks to follow a conservative programme of economic self-help and industrial education. One hundred years later Louis Farrakhan offered African Americans similar advice during the Million Man March on Washington DC. Albeit in black nationalist rhetoric, he called on them to recognise the need for thrift, a stronger work ethic, and a return to family values. 'As the sons of a proud people,' he declared, 'we are coming together and moving forward to chart the course for our future as responsible heads of our families; to reclaim and build our neighborhoods; to unify our families; to save our children who will lead us into the next millennium.'

Today a large section of black society continues to suffer economic and social deprivation. A lack of leadership within the civil rights and black power movements cannot be blamed for this. Moral decay in response to a continued lack of opportunity has been the primary reason for the problems existing today within the melting pot of American society. In 1960, 30 per cent of black babies were born to mothers out of wedlock; in 1995 this number reached an astonishing 70.4 per cent. More than half these children are born into poverty and receive sub-standard education, poor health care, and less than adequate upbringing. To compound this problem, 33 per cent of black males over the age of 20 have criminal records or are currently in prison. And so the cycle continues.

During the first of his televised presidential election debates with Richard Nixon in 1960, Senator John F. Kennedy compared the prospects of black and white American school children. He observed:

> If a Negro baby is born – and this is true also of Puerto Ricans and Mexicans in some of our cities – he has about one-half as much chance to get through high school as a white baby. He has one-third as much chance to get through college as a white student. He has about a third as much chance to be a professional man, about half as much chance to own a house. He has about four times as much chance that he'll be out of work in his life as the white baby. I think we can do better.[1]

Some of the signs are encouraging. Between 1970 and 1995, seven million blacks migrated from inner cities to the suburbs. Indeed, while the white suburban population grew by 63 per cent during this period, the black suburban population increased three times as much – by 193 per cent. At the beginning of the twenty-first century, one-third of all blacks were living in suburbia – twice the proportion 25 years before that.[2] But progress remains slow and, echoing the words of John F. Kennedy, America *will* need to do better.

Notes and references

1 Kevern Verney, *Black civil rights in America*, New York: Routledge, 2000, p. 117.

2 Abigail Thernstrom and Stephan Thernstrom, 'American apartheid? Don't believe it'. *Wall Street Journal*, 2 March 1998.

Select bibliography

The Founding Fathers and civil rights

There are a number of good general texts covering the antebellum period in American history, including James M. McPherson, *Battle cry of freedom – the American Civil War* (Oxford, 1988); Alan Farmer, *The origins of the American Civil War, 1846–1861* (London, 1996); Maldwyn A. Jones, *The limits of liberty – American history, 1607–1980* (Oxford, 1983); Paul S. Boyer *et al.*, *The enduring vision: a history of the American people* (Massachusetts, 1996); and William Loren Katz, *Eyewitness: the negro in American history* (New York, 1967).

Reconstruction

The Army & Navy Gazette (1862–63) and its successor, *The United States Army and Navy Journal* (1863–1950), contain much of value on the work of the Freedmen's Bureau and the impact of the post-Civil War race riots. Other relevant primary sources may be found in John David Smith, *Black voices from Reconstruction, 1865–1877* (Brookfield, 1998). Also see Hans L. Trefousse (ed.), *Background for Radical Reconstruction* (Boston, 1970); Eric Foner, *A short history of Reconstruction* (New York, 1990); and Thomas Holt, *Black over white: negro political leadership in South Carolina during Reconstruction* (Urbana, Illinois, 1977).

Return of white supremacy

For a thorough history of the Ku Klux Klan see Allen W. Trelease, *White terror: the Ku Klux Klan conspiracy and Southern Reconstruction* (Westport, Connecticut, 1971). For other aspects of post-Reconstruction see William Gillette, *Retreat from Reconstruction, 1869–1879* (Baton Rouge, 1979); Lou Falkner Williams, *The great South Carolina Ku Klux Klan trials, 1871–1872* (Georgia, 1996); Stewart E. Tolnay and E. M. Beck, *A festival of violence: an analysis of Southern lynchings, 1882–1930* (Urbana and Chicago, 1992); Stuart Omer Landry, *Battle of Liberty Place: the overthrow of carpet-bag rule in New Orleans* (Baton Rouge, 1999); and Nell Irvin Painter, *Exodusters: black migration to Kansas after Reconstruction* (New York, 1976).

Jim Crow

For a contemporary perspective on the origins of segregation, see C. Vann Woodward, *The strange career of Jim Crow* (New York, 1955). Also of relevance are John R. Howard, *The shifting wind: the Supreme Court and civil rights from Reconstruction to Brown* (New York, 1999); Clifford M. Kuhn, Harlon E. Joye, and E. Bernard West, *Living Atlanta: an oral history of the city, 1914–1948* (Atlanta, Georgia, 1990); Dewey W. Grantham, *Southern progressivism* (Knoxville, Tennessee, 1983); and Patricia McKissack and Fredrick McKissack Jr, *Black diamond: the story of the negro baseball leagues* (New York, 1994). See also Keith Weldon Medley, 'The sad story of how "separate but equal" was born', *Smithsonian*, February 1994.

Early black protest

See Robert Francis Engs, *Educating the disfranchised and disinherited: Samuel Chapman Armstrong and the Hampton Institute, 1839–1893* (Knoxville, Tennessee, 1999); Booker T. Washington, *Up from slavery: an autobiography* (New York, 1901); Booker T. Washington, *The story of my life and work: Booker T. Washington papers* (Toronto, 1901); W. E. B. Du Bois, *The souls of black folk: essays and sketches* (New York, 1969); L. L. Lewis (ed.), *W. E. B. Du Bois: a reader* (New York, 1995); Charles F. Kellog, *History of the National Association for the Advancement of Colored People, 1909–1920* (Baltimore, Maryland, 1967); Alfreda M. Duster *et al.* (eds.), *Crusade for justice: the autobiography of Ida B. Wells* (Chicago, 1970); and J. Stein, *The world of Marcus Garvey: race and class in modern society* (Baton Rouge, 1986).

Impact of war

See Emmett J. Scott, *Scott's official history of the American negro in the world war* (Chicago, 1919); Arthur E. Barbeau and Florette Henri, *The unknown soldiers: black American troops in World War I* (Philadelphia, 1974); John P. Langellier, *American Indians in the US armed forces, 1866–1945* (London, 2000); Spencer R. Crew, *Field to factory: Afro-American migration 1915–1940* (Washington DC, 1987); N. Lemann, *The promised land: the Great Migration and how it changed America* (London, 1991); and Bernard C. Nalty, *Strength for the fight: a history of black Americans in the military* (New York, 1986).

Civil rights in the Cold War

For a contemporary interpretation consult Mary L. Dudziak, *Cold War civil rights* (Princeton, New Jersey, 2000). See also Kevern Verney, *Black civil rights in America* (New York, 2000); R. F. Burk, *The Eisenhower administration and black civil rights* (Knoxville, Tennessee, 1984); C. Carson (ed.), *The autobiography of Martin Luther King* (Boston, 1999); G. B. McKnight, *The last crusade: Martin Luther King, Jr, the FBI, and the poor people's campaign* (Oxford, 1998); T. Branch, *Pillar of fire: America in the King years, 1963–65* (New York, 1998); S. Carmichael and C. V. Hamilton, *Black power: the politics of liberation in America* (London, 1967); and A. Haley (ed.), *The autobiography of Malcolm X* (London, 1968).

Other minority rights

See Howard Zinn, *A people's history of the United States: 1492–present* (New York, 1995); Angelo N. Ancheta, *Race, rights, and the Asian American experience* (New Jersey, 1998); Matt S. Meier and Feliciano Ribera, *The Chicanos: a history of Mexican Americans* (New York, 1972); Alvin M. Josephy Jr, *Red power: the American Indian's fight for freedom* (New York, 1971); Vine DeLoria Jr, *Custer died for your sins: an Indian manifesto* (Oklahoma, 1988); Sheila Rowbotham, *A century of women: the history of women in Britain and the United States* (London, 1997); Samuel Walker, *The rights revolution: rights and community in modern America* (New York, 1998); and Dudley Clendinen and Adam Nagoumey, *Out for good: the struggle to build a gay rights movement in America* (New York, 2001).

Chronology

1776   *4 July:* Declaration of Independence.

1787   Signing of the US Constitution.
Northwest Ordinance.

1791   Bill of Rights.

1793   Fugitive Slave Act.

1812   War with Britain.

1848   Women's rights convention at Seneca Falls, New York.

1861–65   American Civil War.

1863   Emancipation Proclamation.

1865   *3 March:* Freedmen's Bureau established.
14 April: President Abraham Lincoln assassinated.
May: Andrew Johnson begins Presidential Reconstruction.
November: Mississippi enacts the first Black Codes.
6 December: 13th Amendment abolishes slavery.
Congressional Reconstruction begun.

1866   *3 April: Ex parte Milligan* denies freedmen access to the law.
9 April: Civil Rights Act grants blacks citizenship and legal rights.
June: Ku Klux Klan founded.
21 June: Southern Homestead Act.
16 July: Supplementary Freedmen's Bureau Act.

1867   *2 March:* Military Reconstruction Act authorises Federal Army to occupy the South.

1868   *1 April:* Samuel Chapman Armstrong founds the Hampton Institute.
May: National Association for Woman Suffrage founded.
28 July: Burlingame Treaty protects Chinese immigrants from exploitation.
14th Amendment grants citizenship to all born in America.
Freedmen's Bureau terminated (except education).

1869   *February:* 15th Amendment probibits denial of suffrage.
November: American Woman Suffrage Association founded.

1871   *20 April:* Third Enforcement Act (Ku-Klux Act) passed.

1873   Slaughterhouse cases rule that 14th Amendment protects only rights of national citizenship.

1874   *14 September:* Battle of Liberty Place.

1875 *March:* Second Civil Rights Act forbids racial discrimination in public places.
Mississippi Plan initiates white supremacists' campaign in South.
Exoduster 'Pap' Singleton begins black migration to Kansas.
US v. Reese holds that 15th Amendment does not guarantee right to vote.

1876 *US v. Cruikshank* holds that 14th Amendment does not protect individuals from racial crimes unless infringed by state action.

1877 Tilden/Hayes deal ends military occupation of the South
Reconstruction ends.

1878 First 'Jim Crow' law passed in Louisiana.

1881 Booker T. Washington appointed principal of Tuskegee Institute.

1882 Chinese Exclusion Act denies Chinese US citizenship.

1883 Civil rights cases rule that Civil Rights Act of 1875 is unconstitutional.

1887 National Afro-American League founded by T. Thomas Fortune.
American Protective League established by Henry F. Bowers.

1890 National American Woman Suffrage Association (NAWSA) established.

1893 Enforcement laws repealed.

1894 Immigration Restriction League formed.

1895 Booker T. Washington delivers 'Atlanta Compromise' speech.

1896 *18 May: Plessy v. Ferguson* makes segregation in public places legal throughout the United States.

1898 *Williams v. Mississippi* upholds literacy tests and grandfather clause.

1899 *Cumming v. Board of Education* legalises segregation in education.

1901 Publication of *Lynching and the excuse* by Ida B. Wells-Barnett.

1903 Publication of *The souls of black folk* by W. E. B. Du Bois.
Jack Johnson becomes negro heavyweight boxing champion.

1905 Niagra Movement founded under leadership of W. E. B. Du Bois.

1907 *4 February:* 'Gentleman's Agreement' with Japan.

1908 'Gentleman's Agreement' denies Japanese immigrants right to hold US passports.

1909 *12 February:* National Association for the Advancement of Colored People (NAACP) founded.

1910 W. E. B. Du Bois becomes editor of *The Crisis*.

1911 *Heredity in relation to eugenics* by Charles B. Davenport 'rationalises' racism.

1912 Black athlete Howard Porter Drew becomes the 'world's fastest human'.

1914 Marcus Garvey founds the Universal Negro Improvement Association.

1915 *Birth of a nation*, a film by David W. Griffith, released in Hollywood.
November: Ku Klux Klan revived by William J. Simmons.

1917 *6 April:* America enters the First World War.
Segregated officers' training school established at Fort Des Moines, Iowa.
Blacks begin Great Migration to cities in the North.

1918 Harlem Hellfighters fight alongside the French at Château-Thierry and Belleau Wood.
Choctaw 'code-talkers' with American Expeditionary Force in France.

1919 *19–20 July:* 39 people killed in race riots in Washington DC.
19th Amendment provides female suffrage.

1920 *August:* Female suffrage finally ratified.
August: UNIA First International Convention of the Negro Peoples of the World.
Negro National League (baseball) established.

1921 Equal Rights Amendment written by Alice Paul.

1924 *2 June:* Indian Citizenship Act.
Immigration Act bars immigration from China and Japan.

1927 Marcus Garvey deported back to Jamaica.

1929 'National origins' quotas introduced.

1934 Elijah Muhammad becomes leader of Nation of Islam.

1936 Jesse Owens sets seven world athletics records at the Berlin Olympics.

1938 President Roosevelt establishes the Civil Rights Section of the Justice Department.
Missouri ex rel. Gaines v. Canada rules that 'separate' black facilities must be 'equal' to those provided for whites.

1941 *25 June:* President Roosevelt signs Executive Order 8802 prohibiting discrimination in Federal agencies and organisations engaged in the war effort.
7 December: Japanese attack Pearl Harbor and America enters Second World War.
Japanese Americans placed in internment camps.
Blacks enlisted in segregated military units.
Bracero programme allows cheap Mexican labour into America.

1942 *June:* Congress of Racial Equality (CORE) founded.

1945 Cold War begins.

1946 President Truman establishes a committee on civil rights.

1947 *April:* CORE members conduct first 'freedom ride', called 'Journey of Reconciliation'.
10 April: Jackie Robinson becomes first black to play major league baseball.
29 October: To secure these rights report published.

1948 *26 July:* Truman issues Executive Order 9981 officially ending segregation in the US military.

1954 *17 May: Brown v. Board of Education of Topeka, Kansas*, begins integration in public schools.
Hernandez v. Texas represents the first Mexican-American discrimination case to reach the Supreme Court.

1955 *December:* Montgomery bus boycott begins after Rosa Parks refuses to give up her seat.

1956 *21 December:* Montgomery bus boycott ends.

1957 *17 June: Yates v. United States* rules that membership of Communist Party is not a threat to the state.
September: Nine black students barred from school in Little Rock.
Civil Rights Act empowers Justice Department to begin law-suits in voting rights cases.
Southern Christian Leadership Conference (SCLC) formed.

1960 *February:* CORE student 'sit-ins' begin.
16–17 April: Student Non-violent Co-ordinating Committee (SNCC) formed.
Civil Rights Act strengthens 1957 legislation.

1961 President Kennedy issues Executive Order 10925 providing improved employment opportunities in Federal government.

1962 *20 November:* Kennedy issues Executive Order 11063 ending segregation in Federal housing.
Engel v. Vitale prohibits prayer in public schools.
National Farm Workers Association founded.

1963 *28 August:* March on Washington – Martin Luther King Jr delivers 'I have a dream' speech.
22 November: Kennedy assassinated in Dallas, Texas.
Birmingham protests receive international news coverage.
Governor George Wallace blocks integration at University of Alabama.
Presidential Commission on the Status of Women reports on sexual discrimination in employment.
The feminine mystique, by Betty Friedan, published.
Abington Township v. Schempp rules that prayers and Bible-reading in public schools are violations of the constitutional principle of the separation of church from state.

1964 *21 June:* Murder of three civil rights workers in Mississippi.
Freedom Summer.
Civil Rights Act prohibits racial discrimination in all public places in America.
August: Gulf of Tonkin incident commits America to Vietnam War.
Malcolm X forms Organization of Afro-American Unity (OAAU).

1965 *21 February:* Malcolm X assassinated.
7 March: Selma March.
August: riots in the Watts district of Los Angeles.
Voting Rights Act abolishes discrimination against minority voters.
Immigration and Naturalization Act abolishes 'national origins' quota.
Equal Employment Opportunity Commission (EEOC) prohibits employment discrimination.

1966 *October:* Black Panther movement founded in Oakland, California.
2 November: Cuban Adjustment Act allows Cuban migrants to remain in US.
Stokely Carmichael becomes chairman of SNCC.
Cesar Chávez leads grape-pickers march to Sacramento.
National Organization for Women founded.

1967 *29 July:* National Advisory Commission on Civil Disorder (Kerner Commission) established.
Mexican American Youth Organization established.
Mexican American Legal Defense and Education Fund founded.

1968 *March:* Kerner Commission report published.
4 April: Martin Luther King Jr assassinated in Memphis.
Rioting in 130 cities throughout America.
Fair Housing Act prohibits racial discrimination in sale and letting of property.
American Indian Movement (AIM) founded in Minneapolis.

1969 *27 June:* Stonewall Riots bring attention to need for gay rights.
November: Alcatraz Island occupied by Native Americans.
Philadelphia Plan reduces discrimination in employment.

1970 *26 August:* Women's Strike for Equality demonstration in New York.
California Indian Legal Service established.

1971 *20 April:* Busing approved via *Swan v. Charlotte-Mecklenburg Board of Education*.
Giggs v. Duke Power Company upholds 'positive discrimination' in employment.
Congressional Black Caucus established.
National Women's Political Caucus founded.
Native American Rights Fund established to help Indians on a national level.

1972 AIM-backed march on Washington DC.

1973 AIM-backed occupation of Wounded Knee.
Roe v. Wade provides right to abortion.
Vocation Rehabilitation Act ends discrimination against disabled people.

1974 Restore Our Alienated Rights (ROAR) established in Boston as protest against busing.

1975 *Miliken v. Bradley* permits exclusion of Detroit suburbs from integration plan.
Indian Self-determination and Education Assistance Act passed.

1976 Indian Health Care Improvement Act passed.

1978 *Regents of the University of California v. Bakke* upholds the constitutionality of 'affirmative action' but orders that Alan Bakke be admitted to the University of California medical school.
Indian Child Welfare and Indian Religious Acts passed.

1979 *14 October:* Gay and lesbian civil rights march on Washington DC.

1983 American Federation of Labor and Congress of Industrial Organizations (AFL-CIO) vote to support gay rights legislation.

1985 Gay rights demonstration in Washington DC.

1995 Million Man March on Washington DC.

1996 *Romer v. Evans* invalidates the prohibition of gay rights laws.

Index

Abernathy, Reverend Ralph, 87, 90
abortion, right of, 119, 120
Abyssinia, Italian invasion of, 65, 68, 76
Abzug, Bella, 118
Ackerman, Amos T., 32
Adams, John Quincy, 6
Adams, Lewis, 58
affirmative action programmes, 99–100
African Americans: antebellum discrimination
  against free blacks, 4–5, 11, 12; and Black
  Codes, 15–16, 22, 24; and black power,
  97–8, 125; and Black Reconstruction, 23;
  and civil rights movement, 84–8, 90–100;
  and Civil War, 10, 12–13; and Congressional
  Reconstruction, 17–22; early black leaders,
  58–61; Exodusters, 35–7, 42–4, 73; and
  First World War, 70–2, 77–8; and
  Freedmen's Bureau, 19–22, 25–6; and Great
  Migration, 73–4, 79–80; and Jim Crow laws,
  1, 45, 46, 47–57, 58, 86; and Ku Klux Klan,
  30–2, 37–40, 65, 74, 84; lynching of, 31, 35,
  42, 51, 62–3, 67, 72; and organised black
  resistance, 61–5; and progress of civil rights,
  125–6; and Red Shirts, 33–4, 40–1; and
  Revolutionary War, 1, 11; and Second World
  War, 76–7, 80; and segregation in sport,
  51–4, 57; and Supreme Court, 46; and
  Vietnam War, 95–6; and voting rights, 4–5,
  49–50, 90, 93, 94, 95, 104; see also
  education; race riots; slavery
Afro-American Council, 62
agriculture: Mexican agricultural workers,
  113–14, 122; sharecropping, 22; and the
  Tuskegee Normal and Industrial Institute,
  59–60
AIM (American Indian Movement), 115
Alabama: Birmingham protests (1963), 90–1,
  94; integration of University of (1963), 91;
  Montgomery bus boycott, 86–8; Selma
  March (1965), 95, 104; Tuskegee Normal
  and Industrial Institute, 58–60
Alcatraz Island, Native American occupation
  of, 115, 123
American Party (Know-Nothings), 107
American Protective League, 107
Angell, James, 109
Anthony, Susan B., 116, 117
Arkansas, and the 'Little Rock Nine', 84–6,
  100–1

armed forces: and African Americans, 70–2,
  76, 77, 96; ending of segregation, 83
Armstrong, Samuel Chapman, 58, 59, 60
Arthur, President Chester, 109–10
Asian immigrants, 108–11, 112, 121–2
ASWPL (Association of Southern Women for
  the Prevention of Lynching), 62
athletes, African American, 51–2
Atlanta University, 61
AWOC (Agricultural Workers Organizing
  Committee), 113

Baker, Ray Stannard, 50
Bakke, Alan, 100
Banks, Dennis, 115
baseball, racial segregation in, 52–3
Bellecourt, Clyde, 115
Bevel, James, 90
Bill of Rights, 2, 3, 73
Birth of a Nation (film), 74
Black Codes, 15–16, 22, 24
Black Cross, 64
Black Muslims, 97
Black Panthers, 98, 125
black power movement, 97–8, 103, 125
Black Reconstruction, 23, 100
Black Star Line, 64, 65
Blair, Ezell Jr, 88
Bowers, Henry F., 107
boxing, 51
Bradley, Judge Joseph P., 46
Brown, John, 9, 31, 36
Brown, Judge Henry Billings, 47–8
Brown, Linda, 83
Bruce, Louis R., 115
Buchanan, James, 9
Bulge, Battle of the (1944), 77, 80
Burlingame Treaty (1868), 108–9, 110
Burnett, McKinley, 83
Bush, George, 120
Butler, Sergeant William, 72

Cain, Reverend Richard, 23
Calhoun, John C., 7
California: Asian immigrants in, 109, 110; farm
  workers in, 113–14
Carmichael, Stokely, 97, 125
Catholic immigrants, 107
Catt, Carrie Chapman, 116, 117

CBC (Congressional Black Caucus), 100
Chaney, James, 93–4
Chávez, Cesar E., 113, 114
Chicago: migration of African Americans to, 73–4, 80; race riots (1920), 79
Chicanos (Mexican Americans), 112–14
Chinese Exclusion Act (1882), 110
Chinese immigrants, 108–10, 121–2
Chisholm, Shirley, 118
CIC (Council for Interracial Co-operation), 62
Cicero, Marcus Tullius, 2
CILS (California Indian Legal Service), 116
cities, migration to, 106, 114, 126
citizenship: Chinese, 108–10; and Native Americans, 73
Civil Rights Acts: (1866), 17; (1875), 19, 46; (1957), 88–9; (1960), 89; (1964), 91, 94, 118
Civil Rights Commission, 88–9
Civil War (1861–65), 1, 6, 9–10, 14, 45, 116
Clarke, Edward Young, 65
Clay, Henry, 6, 7
Cold War, 76, 82, 117
Colvard, James, 48
communism, and 'rights revolution', 119
Congressional Reconstruction, 17–22
Congressmen, African American, 23, 100
Connor, Eugene 'Bull', 90
Constitution: 13th Amendment (1865), 1, 10, 15; 14th Amendment (1868), 17–18, 23, 46, 49, 50, 113, 116, 118, 119; 15th Amendment (1869), 18–19, 23, 49, 95; 19th Amendment (1918), 117; and Bill of Rights, 2; and Equal Rights Amendment (ERA), 118; and slavery, 2–4; and states' rights to secede from the Union, 6–7
Conway, Captain Thomas W., 19
CORE (Congress of Racial Equality), 86, 87, 88, 89, 91, 93, 113, 125
Costigan–Wagner Bill, 63
cotton growing, and slave trade, 4
Cuban Adjustment Act (1966), 112

Davenport, Dr Charles Benedict, 108
Davis, Judge David, 45
Declaration of Independence, 1, 2, 5
Declaration of the Rights of Man and of the Citizen, 2
Delany, Martin, 10
Democrats: anti-slavery ('Barnburners'), 8; and Ku Klux Klan, 29, 30; and New Deal years, 75–6; in South Carolina, 27; and Southern states, 5, 34, 41–2
Desdunes, Rodolphe, 47
Dewey, Thomas, 83
Dickinson, John, 3
Dillingham Commission (Immigration Commission), 108
disabled people, eliminating discrimination against, 119
Dorsey, George, 82

Douglas, Stephen A., 8
Douglass, Frederick, 10, 37, 61
Du Bois, W.E.B., 58, 60–1, 62, 63, 64–5, 66–7, 70

Eckford, Elizabeth, 85, 100–1
education: and affirmative action programmes, 100; of Asian children, 110; black schools, 97; busing of students, 99; ending of segregation in, 75, 83–4, 88, 90, 91, 99; and Freedmen's Bureau, 20, 21–2; and freedom schools, 93–4; and Jim Crow laws, 48–9; and 'Little Rock Nine', 84–6, 100–1; and 'rights revolution', 119; and Tuskegee Normal and Industrial Institute, 58–60
EEOC (Equal Employment Opportunity Commission), 118
Eisenhower, Dwight D., 84, 88–9, 91, 94
employment: and affirmative action programmes, 99; ending racial discrimination in, 76, 83, 91; sex discrimination in, 117–18
ERA (Equal Rights Amendment), 118
eugenics, 108
Eustis, William, 11
Evans, Hiram Wesley, 74, 80
Exodusters, 35–7, 43–4, 73

Fair Housing Act (1968), 99
Farmer, James, 86, 125
Farrakhan, Louis, 125
Faubus, Orval, governor of Arkansas, 84, 85–6
Federal government, and the Constitution, 2–4
feminism, 117–18
Ferguson, John Howard, 47
Fessenden, William Pitt, 17
First World War, 70–4, 77–8
Forbes, George Washington, 60
Ford, President Gerald, 99
Forrest, Nathan Bedford, 30
Fortune, Thomas T., 60, 61–2
Franklin, Benjamin, 3
Free Soil Party, 8
Freedmen's Bureau, 19–22, 25–6
freedom rides, 86, 88, 92
Freedom Summer project, 93–4, 97
Frémont, John C., 9
Friedan, Betty, *The feminine mystique*, 118

Gaines, Lloyd, 75
Garvey, Marcus, 63, 64–5, 67–8
gay rights, 119–20
George, James Zachariah, 33
German immigrants, 106, 107
Goodman, Andrew, 94
Graham, Dr A.A., 78
Grant, Ulysses S., 29, 32, 33, 34
Greece, Ancient, and concept of civil rights, 1–2

Green, Ernest, 85
Griffith, David W., 74
Grimké sisters, 116
Gutiérrez, José Angel, 113

Haile Selassie, emperor of Abyssinia, 65, 68
Hamilton, Alexander, 3
Harlan, Judge John M., 48, 55
Hastie, Judge William, 77
Hayes, President Rutherford B., 34, 109
health care, and Freedmen's Bureau, 20
Henry, Patrick, 3
Hernandez, Pete, 113
Hill, W.R., 36
Hood, James, 91
Hoover, Herbert, 74, 75
Houser, George, 86
housing, discrimination in, 99, 101
Howard, General Oliver O., 19, 22
Howe, Julia Ward, 116
Hughes, Langston, 103
Hull, Cordell, 77
Hungarian immigrants, 106
Husband, William Walter, 108

immigrants, 106–14, 120–2
Immigration Act (1924), 111
Immigration Commission (Dillingham Commission), 108
Immigration and Naturalization Act (1965), 111–12
Immigration Restriction League, 108
Irish immigrants, 106, 107
Italian immigrants, 106, 107

Jackson, Jesse, 125
Jackson, President Andrew, 4
Japan: 'Gentleman's Agreement' with, 110–11; and Second World War, 111
Jefferson, Thomas, 2, 3, 5, 6
Jewish immigrants, 106
Jim Crow laws, 1, 45, 46, 47–57, 86
Johns, Reverend Vernon, 87
Johnson, President Andrew, 14–15, 17, 18, 19, 21, 24, 45
Johnson, Ed, 63
Johnson, Henry, 72
Johnson, Jack, 51
Johnson, Lyndon Baines, 82, 88, 94–9; and Kerner Commission, 98–9; and Selma March, 95, 104; and Vietnam War, 95–6; and Voting Rights Act (1965), 95
Jones, Mrs Gilbert E., 123–4
Justice Department, Civil Rights Division, 75, 83

Kansas, migration of black people to, 36–7, 42–4
Kansas–Missouri Border War, 8, 9
Kansas–Nebraska Act (1854), 8, 9

Kearney, Dennis, 109
Kellog, William Pitt, 33
Kennedy, John F., 82, 89–93, 94, 111; address to the American nation (11 June 1963), 91, 102; on prospects of black and white American children, 126; and women's rights, 117
Kennedy, Robert, 89, 90
Kerner Commission (1968), 98–9
Kerner, Otto, 99
King, Edward, 23, 27–8
King, Dr Martin Luther Jr, 87, 89, 90, 95, 97; assassination of, 98; 'I have a dream' speech, 93, 102; and Vietnam War, 96
Knights of Labor, 109, 121
Knights of the Nile, 64
Know-Nothings (American Party), 107
Ku Klux Klan, 1, 29–32, 37–40, 46, 65, 74, 80, 84, 107
Ku-Klux Act (1871), 19, 32–3

labour organisations: and Chinese immigrants, 109, 121–2; of farm workers, 113; and gay rights, 120
Langston, John M., 10, 61
Lee, Robert E., 9, 10
legal cases: Brown v. Board of Education of Topeka, Kansas, 48, 83–4, 88; Cumming v. Board of Education, 49, 75; Ex parte Milligan, 45–6; Giggs v. Duke Power Company, 99; Hernandez v. Texas, 113; Miliken v. Bradley case (1975), 99; Missouri ex rel. Gaines v. Canada, 75; Plessy v. Ferguson, 47–8, 54–5; and 'rights revolution', 119, 120; Romer v. Evans, 120; Swan v. Charlotte-Mecklenburg Board of Education, 99; Williams v. Mississippi, 50
Lemley, Judge Harry, 85
Lewis, John, 88, 92
Liberal Party, 8
Liberty Place, Battle of (1874), 33
Lincoln, Abraham, 9, 10, 12–13, 14, 18, 45, 62, 75
Lodge, Henry Cabot, 49
Long, Jefferson, 23
Los Angeles race riots (1965), 97
lynching, 31, 35, 42, 51, 72; organised black resistance against, 62–3, 67

McCain, Franklin, 88
McCarran Walter Act (1952), 111
McCarthy, Senator Joseph, 119
McKinley, President William, 50, 63
McNeil, Joseph, 88
Malcolm X, 97, 98, 103
MALDEF (Mexican American Legal Defense and Education Fund), 113
Malone, Vivian, 91
Marshall, Burke, 90
Marshall, Thurgood, 83, 89

Martinet, Louis, 47
Mason–Dixon line, 6
Meredith, James, 89
Merrill, Major Lewis, 32
Mexican Americans (*Chicanos*), 112–14
Military Reconstruction Act (1867), 18, 30
Milligan, Lambdin P., 45
Mississippi murders (1964), 93–4
Mississippi Plan (1875), 33–4, 41–2
Missouri Compromise (1820), 5–6, 8
Mitchell, George, 115
Montgomery, Isaiah Thornton, 21
Montgomery bus boycott, 86–8
Mott, Lucretia, 116

NAACP (National Association for the
    Advancement of Colored People), 62, 63, 74,
    75, 76, 83, 85, 87, 89, 91, 92, 93, 97, 125
NARF (Native American Rights Fund), 116
Nation of Islam, 125
National Afro-American League, 61
National Origins Act (1929), 111
National Urban League, 74
National Women's Political Caucus, 118
Native Americans, 1, 114–16; and First World
    War, 72–3; occupation of Alcatraz Island,
    115, 123
NAWSA (National American Woman Suffrage
    Association), 116, 117
New Deal, 75–6
New Orleans: and Jim Crow laws, 47, 55–6;
    riots (1866), 16, 17, 24–5; and White League,
    33
Newton, Huey P., 98, 125
NFWA (National Farm Workers Association),
    113
Niagara Movement, 62
Night Walker, 116
Nixon, E.D., 87
Nixon, Richard M., 89, 99–100, 115, 126
Northern states: and Civil War, 10; free blacks
    in, 4–5, 11–13; Great Migration to, 73–4,
    79–80
Northwest Ordinance, 3–4
NOW (National Organization for Women),
    118
nullification crisis, 6–7

OAAU (Organization of Afro-American Unity),
    97
Oakes, Richard, 115
Oklahombi, Joseph, 72
Ovington, Mary White, 50
Owen, Senator Robert L., 123
Owens, Jesse, 52

Parks, Mrs Rosa, 87
Paul, Alice, 118
Pennington, Dr James W.C., 12
Pershing, John J., 71

Philadelphia Plan (1969), 99
Pickens, William, 65
Plessy, Homer, 47–8
poverty, and African Americans, 97, 125–6
Presidential Reconstruction, 14–17, 22
'Progressive' era, 50–1

race riots: and assassination of Martin Luther
    King, 98; in Birmingham, Alabama (1963),
    90–1, 94; in Chicago (1920), 79; and First
    World War, 72; in Harlem (1964), 103; in Los
    Angeles (1965), 97; and Presidential
    Reconstruction, 16–17, 24–5; and Selma
    March (1965), 95, 104; in Springfield, Illinois
    (1908), 62
railroads, and Jim Crow laws, 47–8, 55, 65
Rainey, James, 31
Rainey, Joseph H., 23
Randolph, A. Philip, 65, 76, 91, 92
Reagan, Ronald, 120
Reconstruction, 14–28, 29; Black, 23, 100;
    Congressional, 17–22; end of, 34–5;
    Presidential, 14–17, 22
Red Shirts, 33–4, 40–1
Rehnquist, William H., 120
Republicans: and Ku Klux Klan, 30, 31; and
    Mississippi Plan, 35–6, 41, 42; and
    Reconstruction, 14, 16–17, 19, 29, 30, 34, 35;
    and slavery, 8–9; in South Carolina, 27
Revolutionary War, 1, 11
Rice, Thomas Dartmouth 'Daddy', 45
Richmond, David, 88
Rickey, Branch, 57
'rights revolution', 117, 119, 120
ROAR (Restore Our Alienated Rights)
    campaign, 99
Roberts, Needham, 72
Robeson, Paul, 52
Robinson, Jo Ann, 87
Roosevelt, Franklin D., 75–6, 82
Roosevelt, Theodore, 50–1, 110
Rousseau, Jean-Jacques, 2
Rowan, Carl, 89
Russian immigrants, 106
Rustin, Bayard, 86, 90, 91

Scandinavian immigrants, 106, 107
Schwerner, Michael, 94
scientific racism, 108
SCLC (Southern Christian Leadership
    Conference), 90
Scott, Emmett J., 78
Scott, General Hugh, 72
Scott, Robert K., 32
Seale, Bobby, 98
Second World War, 76–7, 80, 111, 112
Selma March (1965), 95, 104
sharecropping, 22
Shaw, Dr Anna Howard, 116
Sheridan, General Phillip, 24–5

Sherman, William T., 21
Shutterworth, Fred, 90
Sieyès, Emmanuel, 2
Simmons, William J., 74
Singleton, Benjamin 'Pap', 36, 37
Slaughterhouse cases (1873), 46
slave trade, 3, 4
slavery: and Black Codes, 16, 22; and Civil
    War, 9–10, 12–13; and Compromise of 1850,
    7; and Constitution, 2–4; and Emancipation
    Proclamation, 10, 36; and Freedmen's
    Bureau, 21; and 'John Brown' rebellion, 9,
    31, 36; and Missouri Compromise (1820),
    5–6; and Presidential Reconstruction, 14–15;
    and Republicans, 8–9
Smalls, Robert, 23
Smiley, Reverend Glen, 87
Smith, Albert E., 74
SNCC (Student Non-violent Co-ordinating
    Committee), 88, 92, 93, 97, 113, 125
Socrates, 1
South Carolina: and Black Codes, 16;
    Constitutional Convention (1868), 23; and
    Freedmen's Bureau, 21, 25; and Ku Klux
    Klan, 31, 32–3, 39; legislature, 27–8; and
    Reconstruction, 34; Red Shirts in, 40–1
Southern states: and Black Codes, 15–16, 22,
    24; and black voting rights, 4–5, 49–50, 90,
    93, 94, 95, 104; and Civil Rights Acts, 89;
    and Compromise of 1850, 7; and Democrats,
    5, 34, 41–2; and desegregation of schools,
    83–6, 94; and doctrine of 'dual citizenship',
    46; and Great Migration, 73–4, 79–80; and
    Jim Crow laws, 1, 45, 46, 47–9, 54–7; and
    Ku Klux Klan, 1, 29–33, 37–40; and
    lynching, 31, 35, 42, 51, 62–3, 67; and
    Presidential Reconstruction, 14, 15–16; and
    'Progressive era', 50–1; and Reconstruction,
    18–19, 23, 34–5; and Redemption, 35; and
    sharecropping, 22; and 'Tariff of
    Abominations', 6–7; and white supremacy
    activists, 29–35, 74; see also Alabama;
    Arkansas; slavery; South Carolina
sport, racial segregation in, 51–4, 57
Stanton, Elizabeth Cady, 116, 117
Stevens, Thaddeus, 17
Stoic philosophers, 2
Stone, Lucy, 116
Stonewall Riots, 119
Studds, Gerry, 120
student sit-ins, 88
suffrage: and Congressional Reconstruction,
    17–19; disenfranchisement of blacks, 4–5,
    49–50; extension of black voting rights, 90,
    93, 94, 95, 104; and Presidential
    Reconstruction, 15; women's, 116–17,
    123–4
Supreme Court: and affirmative action, 99;
    and civil rights, 45–6, 54–5; and gay rights,
    120; and integrated schools, 83–4, 85; and

the lynching crisis, 63; and right of abortion,
    119; and segregation in interstate travel,
    86
suburban population, and African Americans,
    126

Taft, William, 51
Tallmadge, James, 5–6
Talmadge, Herman, 84
tariffs, and the nullification crisis, 6–7
Texas, migrant agricultural workers in, 122
Thorpe, Grace, 115
Tibbs, Lucy, 16
To secure these rights, 82–3
transport: ending segregation on interstate
    travel, 83, 86; and Montgomery bus boycott,
    86–8; railroads and Jim Crow laws, 47–8,
    55, 65
Trotter, William Monroe, 56, 60
Truman, President Harry S., 76, 82–4, 111
Turner, Henry McNeal, 35–7
Tuskegee Normal and Industrial Institute,
    58–60, 61

unemployment, and African Americans, 97,
    100
UNIA (Universal Negro Improvement
    Association), 64, 65
Universal African Legion, 64

Vardaman, James K., governor of Mississippi,
    49, 56
Vietnam War, 95–6, 118
Villard, Oswald Garrison, 62
Vocation Rehabilitation Act (1973), 119
voting rights, see suffrage
Voting Rights Act (1965), 95

Walker, Francis, 120–1
Wallace, Governor George, 91
Walling, William English, 62
war of 1812, 1
Warren, Chief Justice Earl, 83–4, 113, 119
Washington, Booker T., 20, 50, 58–60, 61, 62,
    63, 64, 66–7; Atlanta Compromise speech,
    60, 65–6, 125
Washington, George, 3
Washington, March on (1963), 88, 91–3
Weaver, Robert C., 89, 101
welfare spending, 100
Wells-Barnett, Ida, 62–3, 67
Whig Party, 5, 8
White League, 33
Whitney, Eli, 4
Wilkes, John, 2
Wilkins, Roy, 89, 92
Wilson, Woodrow, 51, 56–7, 70, 74
Wofford, Harris, 89
women's rights, 1, 116–18, 123–4
Woodward, C. Vann, 48

18271632R00086

Printed in Great Britain
by Amazon